Heaven's Battle Plan

How to Pray Effectively

Maryann Geyser

THIS

PRAYER JOURNAL

belongs to:

_____

Acknowledgements

The completion of *Heaven's Battle Plan: How to Pray Effectively* has been a journey of faith, prayer, and perseverance. I am deeply grateful to the many people whose love, prayers, and encouragement have helped bring this journal to life.

To my husband, **Tommy Geyser**, whose steadfast love and constant encouragement inspired me to keep going—thank you for believing in this vision from the very beginning and for walking this path of faith beside me.

To **Cathy Malone** for your faithful dedication to taking notes over the years. Your diligence and consistency became a foundation upon which much of this work was built.

To the **Saturday Prayer Group**. Thank you for your unwavering devotion to prayer and intercession. Your faithfulness has been both a covering and a continual source of inspiration.

To **Scott Bueling**, bestselling ghostwriter and writing coach. Your gracious help, wisdom, and support throughout this process have been invaluable. Thank you for standing with me and guiding this project with care.

To **Michele Cox**, award-winning, multi-genre author and speaker. I am sincerely thankful for your thoughtful editing, attention to detail, and kind patience in refining the manuscript. Your work brought clarity and beauty to every page.

To **Chris Taylor**, award winning graphic designer. Your creative excellence in designing the cover so perfectly captured the heart of this journal—thank you for bringing such artistry and vision to the project.

And to **Aaron Schnobrich**, for your expertise and dedication in guiding this work through to print. Your professionalism ensured that this vision became a reality.

Each of you played a unique and vital part in bringing *Heaven's Battle Plan: How to Pray Effectively* to completion. May the Lord bless you richly for your faithfulness, your partnership, and your labor of love in advancing His Kingdom.

Introduction

"Praying always with all prayer and supplication in the Spirit, being watchful to this end with all perseverance and supplication for all the saints— and for me, that utterance may be given to me, that I may open my mouth boldly to make known the mystery of the gospel, for which I am an ambassador in chains; that in it I may speak boldly, as I ought to speak." Ephesians 6:18-20

The purpose of this journal isn't to become religious about prayer but rather to become faithful in our responsibility to pray.

Over the years, as a united group of believers, we have come together to pray and have kept minutes of our gatherings. These notes have been insightful, revealing the shared burden of the Holy Spirit and a recurring theme. Our prayers are not individual pleas, but a collective effort to pray for the church, the preparation of the Lord's return, the furtherance of the Gospel, Israel, our country, and individuals with specific needs.

This journal summarizes the times we've spent asking, supplicating, inquiring, and waiting on the Lord. Throughout this journey, we have learned several things:

- **Prayer is hard work.**
- **There is fierce opposition to our prayers;** the enemy tries to frustrate and discourage us. However, we fight the good fight of faith and expect to win.
- **God has provided mighty weapons:** His Word, the name of Jesus, and the Keys of the Kingdom.
- **Songs of triumph must precede us in battle.** They render the enemy powerless as we declare and proclaim God's excellent greatness and His ability to do exceedingly abundantly above all we ask or think.

- **We must believe God and wait patiently for answers to prayer.** Some requests are answered instantly, while others may take weeks, months, years, decades, or even lifetimes. Some answers will only come in eternity. We have experienced many seasons together—times of instant answers and blessings, as well as times when it felt like God was silent. However, through it all, we've learned to trust God's plan.

- **Prayer is a way of life that we must commit to,** even when we are unable to gather, it is essential to pray privately at home. However, when we come together, we must consider one another and strive for unity. We see ourselves as an orchestra, playing various instruments, with the Holy Spirit leading and directing us, keeping us connected to our Head, the Lord Jesus.

- **God has placed us in a unique position.** We are on earth but also seated with Him in heavenly places. This means we are always above our circumstances, and our eyes are opened to the spiritual battles we face. To navigate these challenges, we must study God's Word, remain disciplined and teachable, and leave our burdens with the Lord so that we can take up His burdens.

As you commit yourself to spending quality time with the Lord and prepare your heart to receive insights into His nature and character, you will discover the richness of His Word. As you open the Scriptures, you will uncover the depth of God's promises and weave these truths into your prayers. Your faith will grow stronger, and you will flourish.

Invite the Holy Spirit to guide your thoughts and actions, and to empower you with His strength. Take hold of the spiritual tools God has placed in your hands and stand firm on His unshakable promises.

He provides comfort, peace, and strength for every step along the way.

Whenever possible, seek out a prayer partner or join a prayer group, and share in the joy and power of united prayer. From experience, we have found that the more time we devote to prayer, the greater the responsibilities God entrusts to us. Embracing these responsibilities becomes a profound honor as we seek to live in obedience to His will.

Guide to Using This Journal

Before You Begin

Before we step into this 52-week journey of prayer, it is important to pause and learn from the greatest examples we have in Scripture. Prayer was at the very heart of Jesus' life and ministry—He lived in constant communion with His Father, drawing strength, wisdom, and direction through intimate fellowship. Paul, too, demonstrated a life saturated in prayer, interceding for the Church, seeking God's will, and contending for the advancement of the Gospel.

These two studies—**The Prayer Life of Jesus** and **The Prayer Life of Paul**—lay a strong foundation for the weeks ahead. As you reflect on their examples, allow the Holy Spirit to shape your understanding of prayer, deepen your hunger for God's presence, and align your heart with His purposes before beginning this journey.

This journal is designed to lead you through **52 weeks of guided prompts** that deepen your walk with God, strengthen your prayer life, and help you record His faithfulness along the way.

Each week includes the same five sections, creating a consistent rhythm of Scripture, prayer, and reflection.

The Five Weekly Sections

1. Weekly Scripture Focus
Read and reflect on a Bible verse or passage. Pause and allow the Holy Spirit to highlight words or thoughts that stand out to you. Record your reflections, insights, or questions.

Example: Week One might ask, *"Why did Jesus come as a bond servant?"*

2. Prayer for the Church
Lift up your **local church, leaders**, and the **global Body of Christ**. Ask God to strengthen His people and guide them in His purposes. As you pray, write down any declarations, Scriptures, or impressions the Holy Spirit gives you.

Example: A prophetic word, a proclamation, or an encouragement for the church.

3. Prayer for the Great Commission
Pray for the advancement of God's Kingdom worldwide:

- Missionaries and evangelism efforts

- Unreached people groups

- The peace of Jerusalem

- Salvation of the Jewish people to know their Messiah — Jesus

4. Prayer for Others
Intercede for family, friends, and anyone God places on your heart. Record their names, specific needs, and any encouraging words or Scriptures the Holy Spirit gives you. Act on these prompts by sharing encouragement or support when led.

5. Personal Prayer
Your needs matter deeply to God. Bring your requests, burdens, and desires before Him. Use this section to:
- Ask, seek, and knock with faith

- Record promises God gives you

- Note answered prayers and moments of thanksgiving
  This section will become a beautiful record of God's
  faithfulness in your life.

Tips for Using the Journal

- **Start with the Word**

  Begin each week by focusing on the Scripture passage. Meditate on it and allow God to speak before you begin writing and praying.

- **Write Freely**

  This is your personal conversation with God — be honest, open, and authentic.

- **Date Your Entries**

  Mark each prayer and reflection to track God's answers and the Holy Spirit's leading over time.

- **Look Back Often**

  Review past weeks to see God's faithfulness, answered prayers, and how He has moved in your life and the lives of others.

- **Listen for His Voice**

  At the close of each week, in the personal prayer section, take a few quiet moments to meditate. Still your heart, set aside distractions, and allow the Lord to speak gently into your life."

This guide will help you use the journal intentionally, creating a lasting record of **prayer, revelation, and God's transforming work** in your life.

The Prayer Life of Jesus

"Lord, teach us to pray." Luke 11:1

Jesus was a man of prayer who devoted time each day to converse with His Father. He returned to God not to seek any gifts or favors, but simply for the sake of fellowship. His prayer life serves as our example; however, the most significant moments of it occurred away from the eyes of others, in solitude with His Father.

Prayer was an essential part of His life, no matter the circumstances. He experienced joy and sorrow, smiles and tears, ecstasy and weariness. Through it all, He frequently returned to fellowship with His Father, the one He loved most in heaven and on earth. He could not bear to be apart from Him and took every opportunity, day and night, to communicate with Him. Because of this deep communion, His countenance glowed; the fellowship they shared was deeply profound. Luke described one such moment: *"As He prayed, the appearance of His face was altered."*

Luke 9:29

He got up before sunrise, often exhausted from the prior days' ministry, but His strength came from the Father, and His ministry flowed directly from the time He spent with Him in prayer. Mark notes that it was His daily practice: *"Now in the morning, having risen a long while before daylight, He went out and departed to a solitary place; and there He prayed."* Mark 1:35

He prayed alone: *"So He Himself often withdrew into the wilderness and prayed."* Luke 5:16 Sometimes, it is essential for us to get alone with God without distractions and allow Him to speak.

"Be still, and know that I am God." Psalm 46:10

He spent entire nights in prayer: *"And when He had sent them away, He departed to the mountain to pray."* Mark 6:46

He prayed with others: *"He took Peter, John, and James and went up on the mountain to pray,"*

Luke 9:28

Christians are encouraged to pray with one another: *"These all continued together with one accord in prayer and supplication ..."* Acts 1:14

He prayed for individuals: *"And the Lord said, "Simon, Simon! Indeed, Satan has asked for you, that he may sift you as wheat. But I have prayed for you, that your faith should not*

fail; and when you have returned to Me, strengthen your brethren." Luke 22:31-32

But he said to Him, *"Lord, I am ready to go with You, both to prison and to death."*

Then He said, *"I tell you, Peter, the rooster shall not crow this day before you will deny three times that you know Me."* Luke 22:33

He prayed for the children: *"Then little children were brought to Him that He might put His hands on them and pray."* Matthew 19:13

He prayed for Judas, and only God and Jesus know how He wrestled in prayer for Judas's soul.

He prayed for strength in Gethsemane, as the power of darkness closed in on Him, and the temptation to desert God's high road grew fierce: *"Being in agony, He prayed."* Luke 22:44

He prayed to His Father as He hung on the cross for his enemies: *"Then Jesus said, 'Father, forgive them, for they do not know what they do.' And they divided His garments and cast lots."* Luke 23:34

He prayed to His Father as He hung on the cross, His strength almost gone:

"Into Your hands I commit My spirit." Luke 23:46 He died speaking to His Father.

The disciples, inspired by the unique nature of Jesus' prayers, eagerly sought to learn from Him. Some were John the Baptist's disciples, and they had seen Him pray. Many grew up in simple Hebrew homes, no doubt, Peter, Andrew, James, and John learned to say their prayers at their mother's knee, but when Jesus prayed, it was different, and so they asked Him to teach them to pray, and He introduced His disciples to the discipline of prayer.

> *"In this manner, therefore, pray: Our Father in heaven, hallowed be Your name.*
>
> *Your kingdom come, Your will be done on earth, as it is in heaven.*
>
> *Give us this day our daily bread.*
>
> *And forgive us our debts, as we forgive our debtors.*
>
> *And do not lead us into temptation, but deliver us from the evil one. For Yours is the kingdom and the power and the glory forever. Amen."* Matthew 6:9-13

He taught them to be persistent in prayer, using a parable to show them that they should always pray and not give up. Luke 18:1 Persistence is all about timing, He knew that not all His prayers would be answered as expected; He cried out to God the Father from Gethsemane three times to allow an easier path, but said, *"Nevertheless, not as I will, but as You will."* Matthew 26:39

He prayed for Himself, His immediate disciples, as well as for all believers and the world, and based His prayers on His knowledge of God and His truth, and said, *"God is Spirit, and those who worship Him must worship in spirit and in truth."* John 4:24 He also said, *"The truth shall make you free"* in John 8:32, underscoring the importance of truth.

Jesus came to illuminate the profound truth that fellowship with God is not only attainable but also vital for cultivating a meaningful relationship with Him. He made this possible by dying on the cross, preparing the way with love and intention. As our mediator, He opens the door to God's presence, inviting us to approach Him boldly without fear. In this sacred space, we can find mercy and grace that flows from the heart of our Heavenly Father, who embraces us as His cherished children.

In God's presence, we discover a profound sense of peace and joy that transcends our circumstances, offering solace to our weary hearts. He invites us to bring our requests to Him, trusting in His wisdom and mercy. God hears us, granting insights into His desires and intentions. This intimacy empowers us to fulfill God's will on earth, reflects the beauty and harmony of His kingdom and aligns us with His eternal purpose.

What an honor!

The Prayer Life of Paul

When Saul encountered the transformative power of God, he was changed. He recognized himself as "the chief of sinners." However, through God's grace was transformed and given a new name: Paul. As Paul embraced his new identity, his desire for God grew immensely, and empowered by the Holy Spirit, he urged fellow believers to follow his example as he followed Christ. His devotion to God and His Church, drove him to a lifestyle of prayer.

"You are always in my prayers," he often tells them in letters he writes.

"For God is my witness, whom I serve with my spirit in the gospel of His Son, that without ceasing I make mention of you always in my prayers." Romans 1:9

He wrote personal letters to the Roman Christians and the churches in Ephesus, Philippi, Corinth, Colossae, and Thessalonica. Every church except Galatia, received the assurance that he was praying for them. Individual disciples, Timothy and Philemon also received letters informing them of his prayers. He encouraged them to develop a prayer life by saying, "Pray without ceasing" and "Give thanks in all circumstances." 1 Thessalonians 5:17

His prayer for the Church was that Christ would be formed in them, and that they would be rooted and grounded in the faith. His prayer for Israel was that they be saved. His prayers for individuals were frequent and urgent, as he appealed to God for seemingly impossible things. His prayer for the world was that the gospel of Jesus Christ would change them. All his prayers were filled with praise and thanksgiving to God for His ability to keep believers from slipping and falling. He expressed gratitude to God for His grace, asking for spiritual knowledge, strength, and an increase in faith, particularly for young believers.

These passages paint a picture of a man who truly lived by the words *"pray without ceasing."* He understood that young believers required God's grace and power to overcome the enemy's opposition to their salvation, and he prayed for them continually, both day and night. For him, prayer was neither a duty nor a burden; it was the natural inclination of his heart towards God for His work. Thus, he prayed frequently and earnestly, confidently asking for impossible things, affirming that God was capable of providing.

- For the Church in Ephesus, he asked God to give them wisdom, enlightenment, and revelation knowledge of the inheritance they possessed in Christ.

- For the Church in Philippi, Paul requested spiritual knowledge and assistance to live a blameless and fruitful life that would glorify God.

- For the Church in Colossae, he asked for spiritual knowledge, understanding of God's will, and for strength, patience, and joy.

- For the Church in Thessalonica, he prayed that God would increase their love for one another, establish their hearts in holiness, and preserve them.

Paul lived in a heavenly realm; he was at home in the holiness and omnipotence of God and His love, and his prayers reflected this close relationship. He believed that God could and would establish the hearts of other believers. He wanted them to place their trust in God alone, which is why he emphasized the importance of continuous prayer.

Paul's request for prayer for himself is equally instructive. It demonstrated that he did not view prayer as a special privilege reserved for apostles; rather, he encouraged even the humblest and simplest believers to claim their right to pray. He believed that prayer was necessary for everyone, not just new converts or weak Christians, and he depended on the prayers of his fellow believers, even after preaching the gospel for twenty years. He repeatedly asked them to pray for him,

18

so that he could speak as he ought, and urged them to pray for him continually.

"Praying always with all prayer and supplication in the Spirit for all the saints, and for me, that utterance may be given to me, that I may open my mouth boldly to make known the mystery of the gospel." Ephesians 6:18

"For I know that this will turn out for my deliverance through your prayer and the supply of the Spirit of Jesus Christ." Philippians 1:19

"Continue earnestly in prayer, being vigilant in it with thanksgiving; that God would open to us a door for the word, to speak the mystery of Christ, that I may make it manifest as I ought to speak." Colossians 4:2-4

"Brethren, pray for us." 1 Thessalonians 5:25

Christ taught His disciples to pray, and Paul taught the churches to pray. As much as he looked to the Lord in Heaven, he looked to his brethren on earth. The Holy Spirit from Heaven and the prayers on earth are inseparably linked, and everything depends upon getting our supply from the Holy Spirit, for we are powerless without Him. It is Christ's divine order and the Spirit's enabling for all of God's work, and it is His power and commissioning that gives us confidence.

Four Amazing Prayer Requests:

1. A prayer for spiritual strength.

    "That He would grant you, according to the riches of His glory, to be strengthened with might through His Spirit in the inner man." Ephesians 3:16

2. A prayer for Christ to dwell in our hearts.

    "That Christ may dwell in your hearts through faith; that you, being rooted and grounded in love, may be able to comprehend with all the saints what is the width and length and depth and height—to know the love of Christ which passes knowledge; that you may be filled with all the fullness of God." Ephesians 3:17-19

3. A prayer for intimate knowledge of the love of Christ.

"That Christ may dwell in your hearts through faith; that you, being rooted and grounded in love, may be able to comprehend with all the saints what is the width and length and depth and height—to know the love of Christ which passes knowledge; that you may be filled with all the fullness of God." Ephesians 3:17-19

4. A prayer for God's fullness and living in the dimensions of Christ's love.

"That Christ may dwell in your hearts through faith; that you, being rooted and grounded in love, may be able to comprehend with all the saints what is the width and length and depth and height—to know the love of Christ which passes knowledge; that you may be filled with all the fullness of God." Ephesians 3:17-19

These four prayers encompass the width length, height, and depth of Christ's love.

The width of His love includes all humanity.

The length of His love goes on into eternity and forever.

The height of His love picks us up and delivers us from sin and death, making us heirs of salvation.

The depth of His love is revealed in the sacrifice of His Son and the humiliation, suffering, and death Jesus endured because He loves mankind. No one is too wicked or too depraved to receive the love of God.

The prayer lives of Jesus and Paul are not just historical accounts to admire—they are divine invitations to follow. Jesus showed us the heart of intimacy with the Father, and Paul demonstrated the power of persistent, Spirit-led intercession. Their examples call us to cultivate our own deep, personal prayer relationship with God.

Prayer is not optional; it is essential. It is the lifeline of our Christian walk, the place where our hearts align with His will and our lives are transformed by His presence.

Weekly Scripture Focus

"Let this mind be in you, which was also in Christ Jesus, who, being in the form of God, did not consider it robbery to be equal with God, but made Himself of no reputation, taking the form of a bondservant, and coming in the likeness of men." Philippians 2:5-7

As your prayer begins this week, lift up praise to God for His recent provision, and repent of wrongdoing—praying on behalf of yourself, others, the Church, and your nation.

_____

_____

_____

_____

_____

_____

_____

_____

_____

_____

_____

_____

_____

_____

_____

_____

_____

_____

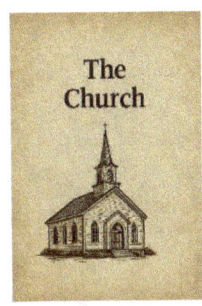

The Church

Pray that we would grow in spiritual maturity—moving beyond spiritual infancy and embracing a deeper walk with God marked by understanding, obedience, and discernment.

Ask the Lord to shape us as believers into the image of Christ, developing His character within us so that we become steadfast, fruitful disciples who reflect His nature in our thoughts, words, and actions.

_____

_____

_____

_____

_____

_____

_____

_____

_____

_____

_____

_____

_____

_____

_____

_____

The Great Commission

Pray for missionaries around the world—that God would cover them with divine protection, supply every need, and strengthen them in their calling.

Ask the Lord to open the eyes of the people they are sent to, that they would become disillusioned with false and demonic gods and turn to the living Christ in repentance and faith.

Pray that the light of the Gospel would pierce every stronghold of darkness.

Pray for the salvation of the Jewish people, and that all those who seek to harm them would be brought to confusion and repentance.

_____

_____

_____

_____

_____

_____

_____

_____

_____

_____

_____

_____

_____

_____

Prayer for Others

Choose someone you know to pray for this week.

Ask God to meet them at their point of need— whether physical, emotional, or spiritual. Pray that His presence would surround them, His provision would sustain them, and His love would draw them closer to Him.

_____

_____

_____

_____

_____

_____

_____

_____

_____

_____

_____

_____

_____

_____

_____

_____

_____

_____

_____

Pray that Christ would be the ultimate prize and the highest goal of your life—above every ambition, desire, or pursuit.

Ask the Holy Spirit to align your heart so that knowing Him, loving Him, and becoming like Him becomes your greatest joy.

_____

_____

_____

_____

_____

_____

_____

_____

_____

_____

_____

_____

_____

_____

_____

_____

_____

_____

_____

Weekly Scripture Focus

"For I was hungry, and you gave Me food; I was thirsty, and you gave Me drink; I was a stranger and you took Me in; I was naked, and you clothed Me; I was sick and you visited Me; I was in prison and you came to Me.

Then the righteous will answer Him, saying, 'Lord, when did we see You hungry and feed You, or thirsty and give You drink? When did we see You a stranger and take You in, or naked and clothe You? Or when did we see You sick, or in prison, and come to You?' And the King will answer and say to them, 'Assuredly, I say to you, inasmuch as you did it to one of the least of these My brethren, you did it to Me." Matthew 25:35-40

As your prayer begins this week, lift up praise to God for His recent provision, and repent of wrongdoing—praying on behalf of yourself, others, the Church, and your nation.

_____

_____

_____

_____

_____

_____

_____

_____

_____

_____

_____

_____

_____

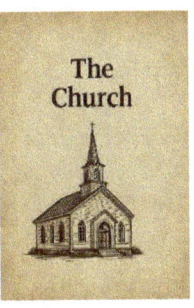

The Church

Pray that we would genuinely love and care for one another—bearing one another's burdens and walking in compassion, just as Christ has loved us.

Esteeming others above ourselves and cultivating humility and selflessness in our words and actions.

The Great Commission

Pray that missionaries sent to difficult and unreached regions would bear much fruit, establishing strong, Spirit-filled churches that will stand as beacons of truth.

Ask God to open doors that no man can shut, and to confirm His Word with signs, wonders, and a powerful manifestation of His presence.

Pray for the salvation of the Jewish people, and that all those who seek to harm them would be brought to confusion and repentance.

_____

_____

_____

_____

_____

_____

_____

_____

_____

_____

_____

_____

_____

_____

_____

_____

_____

Prayer for Others

Ask the Holy Spirit to place someone specific on your heart this week.

Commit to lifting them up in prayer daily asking God to meet their deepest needs, encourage their spirit, and reveal His love and purpose in their life.

Ask the Holy Spirit to increase your faith so that you may trust God fully and stand firm on His promises.

Pray that He will continue and complete the good work He has begun in you, shaping you into the image of Christ.

Thank Him for all He has already done for you.

_____

_____

_____

_____

_____

_____

_____

_____

_____

_____

_____

_____

_____

_____

_____

_____

_____

_____

Weekly Scripture Focus

"Be anxious for nothing, but in everything by prayer and supplication, with thanksgiving, let your requests be made known to God; and the peace of God, which surpasses all understanding, will guard your hearts and minds through Christ Jesus." Philippians 4:6-7

As your prayer begins this week, lift up praise to God for His recent provision, and repent of wrongdoing—praying on behalf of yourself, others, the Church, and your nation.

_____

_____

_____

_____

_____

_____

_____

_____

_____

_____

_____

_____

_____

_____

_____

_____

_____

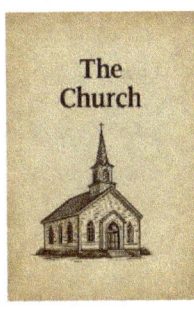

The Church

Pray that we will remain steadfast and fervent in praying for one another, bearing each other's burdens in the spirit of Christ.

Ask that the peace of God would rule in our hearts, guarding our minds and emotions through Christ Jesus.

Pray that we would not be anxious about the future, but that our trust in God's faithfulness would grow stronger each day.

_____

_____

_____

_____

_____

_____

_____

_____

_____

_____

_____

_____

_____

_____

_____

_____

The Great Commission

The Native American Indians are a people deeply rooted in tradition and tribal culture. Many live in conditions of abject poverty, and alcohol and substance abuse are often used to mask their pain.

Pray that God would send workers into this harvest field, for the Gospel has the power to liberate people from darkness.

Ask God to set them free from the bondage of false gods and to bring them into the light of His truth.

_____

_____

_____

_____

_____

_____

_____

_____

_____

_____

_____

_____

_____

_____

_____

_____

Prayer for Others

Choose a family to pray for.

Ask God to give you prophetic insight to pray effectively. Pray for each one specifically. Ask God to protect and provide for them, give them wisdom, and keep them from the attacks of the enemy.

Ask God to give you a word of encouragement to remind them of His love for them.

_____

_____

_____

_____

_____

_____

_____

_____

_____

_____

_____

_____

_____

_____

_____

_____

_____

_____

_____

Ask the Holy Spirit to increase your faith, so that you trust God fully and stand firm on His promises.

Pray that He will continue and complete the good work He has begun in you, to shape you into the image of Christ.

Thank Him for all He has already done.

_____

_____

_____

_____

_____

_____

_____

_____

_____

_____

_____

_____

_____

_____

_____

_____

_____

_____

_____

Weekly Scripture Focus

"And I also say to you that you are Peter, and on this rock I will build My church, and the gates of Hades shall not prevail against it." Matthew 16:18

As your prayer begins this week, lift up praise to God for His recent provision, and repent of wrongdoing—praying on behalf of yourself, others, the Church, and your nation.

_____

_____

_____

_____

_____

_____

_____

_____

_____

_____

_____

_____

_____

_____

_____

_____

_____

_____

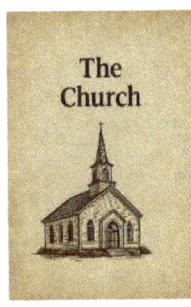

The Church

Thank Jesus for the promise *"I will build my Church, and the gates of Hades shall not prevail against it."* Matthew 16:18

Thank Him for His Word that guides, convicts, and transforms, and leads us in righteousness revealing His will.

Thank Him for the liberty we have in Christ—freedom from sin, shame, and fear.

_____

_____

_____

_____

_____

_____

_____

_____

_____

_____

_____

_____

_____

_____

_____

_____

_____

The Great Commission

Pray that missionaries sent to difficult and unreached regions would bear much fruit, establishing strong, Spirit-filled churches that will stand as beacons of truth.

Ask God for open doors to spread the Gospel, and to confirm His Word through signs, wonders, and a powerful manifestation of His presence.

_____

_____

_____

_____

_____

_____

_____

_____

_____

_____

_____

_____

_____

_____

_____

_____

_____

_____

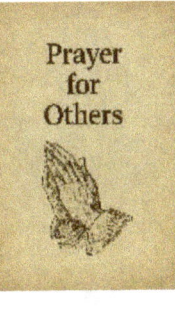

Prayer for Others

Ask the Lord to heal any broken relationships in your family, and to strengthen the bond of love, trust, and unity. If any family members do not yet know Christ, intercede for their salvation, that their hearts may be softened and their eyes opened to the truth of the Gospel.

Ask the Holy Spirit to keep your heart burning with passion and perseverance in prayer—for the Church to be strengthened, for the lost to be saved, and for Israel to fulfill her divine destiny.

"O LORD, our LORD, how excellent is Your name in all the earth, who have set Your glory above the heavens!

Out of the mouth of babes and nursing infants You have ordained strength, Because of Your enemies, That You may silence the enemy and the avenger.

When I consider Your heavens, the work of Your fingers, the moon and the stars, which

You have ordained,

What is man that You are mindful of him, and the son of man that You visit him? For You have made him a little lower than the angels, and You have crowned him with glory and honor.

You have made him to have dominion over the works of Your hands;

You have put all things under his feet." Psalm 8:1-6

As your prayer begins this week, lift up praise to God for His recent provision, and repent of wrongdoing—praying on behalf of yourself, others, the Church, and your nation.

The Church

God inhabits the praises of His people. As we praise, the enemy is silenced and bound, and we execute the written judgments of God against all forces of darkness. There is power in praise!

Declare Boldly:

- Our God reigns over every situation—He is sovereign and victorious!
- God's Word prevails, even in what seems impossible—nothing is too hard for Him!

_____

_____

_____

_____

_____

_____

_____

_____

_____

_____

_____

_____

_____

_____

The Great Commission

Pray for the conviction of the Holy Spirit, when the Gospel is preached from pulpits around the country.

Pray for many salvations and changed lives.

Pray especially for people who will respond to the Gospel.

_____

_____

_____

_____

_____

_____

_____

_____

_____

_____

_____

_____

_____

_____

_____

_____

_____

_____

Prayer for Others

Choose a new believer to pray for, ask God to help them stand firm in their decision.

Pray that they will receive the Word with gladness and that they will grow.

Pray that they would have a hunger for God's Word, follow Christ, become a true disciple, and a fisher of men.

_____

_____

_____

_____

_____

_____

_____

_____

_____

_____

_____

_____

_____

_____

_____

_____

_____

Ask God for a fresh, daily infilling of His Holy Spirit, as instructed in Ephesians 5:18.

Pray for a life of consecration and holiness, that your heart may remain sensitive and ready to hear His voice whenever He speaks.

_____

_____

_____

_____

_____

_____

_____

_____

_____

_____

_____

_____

_____

_____

_____

_____

_____

_____

Weekly Scripture Focus

"God is Spirit, and those who worship Him must worship in spirit and truth." John 4:24

"For even if there are so-called gods, whether in heaven or on earth (as there are many gods and many lords), yet for us there is one God, the Father, of whom are all things, and we for Him; and one Lord Jesus Christ, through whom are all things, and through whom we live." 1 Corinthians 8:5-6

"He who dwells in the secret place of the Most High shall abide under the shadow of the Almighty.

I will say of the LORD, He is my refuge and my fortress; my God, in Him I will trust." Psalm 91:1-2

As your prayer begins this week, lift up praise to God for His recent provision, and repent of wrongdoing—praying on behalf of yourself, others, the Church, and your nation.

_____

_____

_____

_____

_____

_____

_____

_____

_____

_____

_____

_____

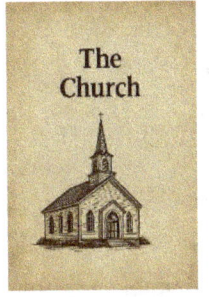

The Church

Pray that as believers, we would walk in obedience to God's Word, giving it first place in our hearts and lives.

Pray that we would serve the Lord joyfully and wholeheartedly, honoring Him in all we do.

Pray that no foreign gods, idols, or distractions would take root among us—only wholehearted devotion to the Lord.

_____
_____
_____
_____
_____
_____
_____
_____
_____
_____
_____
_____
_____
_____
_____
_____
_____

The Great Commission

Pray for those living in nations where the Gospel is forbidden.

Ask God to strengthen and sustain the underground Church.

Pray for divine protection over those who smuggle Bibles and Christian materials into restricted regions.

Intercede for missionaries who risk their lives to shine the light of Christ. Ask the Lord to give them courage, wisdom, and supernatural favor.

_____

_____

_____

_____

_____

_____

_____

_____

_____

_____

_____

_____

_____

_____

_____

_____

_____

Prayer for Others

Pray for unsaved loved ones and friends,

"Whose minds the god of this age has blinded, who do not believe, lest the light of the gospel of the glory of Christ, who is the image of God, should shine on them." 2 Corinthians 4:4

Ask God to remove the blindfolds.

Meditate on the name of Jesus—the name that is above every other name.

Reflect on all that He means to you: Savior, Redeemer, Friend, Healer, and Lord.

Thank the Father for the gift of His Son, and for the power and authority found in His Name—a name that grants you access to the very throne room of God.

Weekly Scripture Focus

"Therefore if the Son makes you free, you shall be free indeed." John 8:36

"There is therefore now no condemnation to those who are in Christ Jesus, who do not walk according to the flesh, but according to the Spirit. For the law of the Spirit of life in Christ Jesus has made me free from the law of sin and death." Romans 8:1-2

"But He was wounded for our transgressions, He was bruised for our iniquities; The chastisement for our peace was upon Him, And by His stripe we are healed." Isaiah 53:5

"Come to Me, all you who labor and are heavy laden, and I will give you rest." Matthew 11:28

As your prayer begins this week, lift up praise to God for His recent provision, and repent of wrongdoing—praying on behalf of yourself, others, the Church, and your nation.

_____

_____

_____

_____

_____

_____

_____

_____

_____

_____

_____

The Church

Ask God to knit our hearts together in love – one heart, one mind, walking in harmony, free from division, united in purpose as the Body of Christ.

Pray that we would reflect the character of Christ and bring glory to God's name. Ask the Holy Spirit to give us a greater understanding of the finished work of the cross, the victory over sin and death and the freedom and authority Christ has won for us.

_____

_____

_____

_____

_____

_____

_____

_____

_____

_____

_____

_____

_____

_____

_____

_____

_____

The Great Commission

Pray earnestly for the peace of Jerusalem.

Ask the Holy Spirit to grant you insight— on how to intercede effectively.

Stay watchful of current events in the news, using them as prayer prompts.

Pray for the salvation of the Jewish people, and that all those who seek to harm them would be brought to confusion and repentance.

Prayer for Others

Pray for your co-workers, especially those who do not know Christ.

Ask God to soften their hearts and prepare a way for the Gospel to reach them.

Pray for divine opportunities to share your faith with boldness, love, and wisdom, and that your life would be a living testimony of God's grace in the workplace.

_____

_____

_____

_____

_____

_____

_____

_____

_____

_____

_____

_____

_____

_____

_____

_____

_____

_____

Pray against all forms of deception in your life.

Ask God to give you discernment and to keep you spiritually alert, steadfast in truth, and always on guard. Pray that you remain attentive to His voice and quick to obey His leading without hesitation.

_____

_____

_____

_____

_____

_____

_____

_____

_____

_____

_____

_____

_____

_____

_____

_____

_____

_____

_____

Weekly Scripture Focus

"Again, I say to you that if two of you agree on earth concerning anything that they ask, it will be done for them by My Father in heaven." Matthew 18:19

"There is neither Jew nor Greek, there is neither slave nor free, there is neither male nor female; for you are all one in Christ Jesus." Galatians 3:28

As your prayer begins this week, lift up praise to God for His recent provision, and repent of wrongdoing—praying on behalf of yourself, others, the Church, and your nation.

_____

_____

_____

_____

_____

_____

_____

_____

_____

_____

_____

_____

_____

_____

_____

_____

The Church

Pray that we would be united in heart and mind, fully participating and coming into agreement with the Lord concerning His will—carrying faithfully the burdens of intercession for others.

_____

_____

_____

_____

_____

_____

_____

_____

_____

_____

_____

_____

_____

_____

_____

_____

_____

_____

_____

The Great Commission

Pray for revival.

"If My people who are called by My name, will humble themselves, and pray and seek My face, and turn from their wicked ways, then I will hear from heaven, and will forgive their sin and heal their land." 2 Chronicles 7:14

Pray for the peace of Jerusalem.

_____

_____

_____

_____

_____

_____

_____

_____

_____

_____

_____

_____

_____

_____

_____

_____

_____

_____

_____

_____

Prayer for Others

Choose a young person and begin to stand in the gap for them.

Ask God to anchor them in unshakable faith, ignite a passion for truth within their heart, and raise them up as a light in the midst of a dark generation.

Pray that they would be bold, Spirit-filled witnesses—fearless in their stand for Christ and influential among their peers. Intercede for their spiritual growth, that they may walk in wisdom, courage, and the power of the Holy Spirit.

_____

_____

_____

_____

_____

_____

_____

_____

_____

_____

_____

_____

_____

_____

_____

_____

_____

_____

Ask God to fill you with wisdom and spiritual understanding.

Pray for ears that are attentive to His voice and eyes that perceive His work in the earth today. Ask the Holy Spirit to make you alert, discerning and prepared for the return of the Lord.

_____

_____

_____

_____

_____

_____

_____

_____

_____

_____

_____

_____

_____

_____

_____

_____

_____

_____

_____

Weekly Scripture Focus

"Set your mind on things above, not on things on the earth." Colossians 3:2

"For I consider that the sufferings of this present time are not worthy to be compared with the glory which shall be revealed in us." Romans 8:18

"And we know that all things work together for good to those who love God, to those who are the called according to His purpose." Romans 8:28

As your prayer begins this week, lift up praise to God for His recent provision, and repent of wrongdoing—praying on behalf of yourself, others, the Church, and your nation.

_____

_____

_____

_____

_____

_____

_____

_____

_____

_____

_____

_____

_____

_____

_____

_____

_____

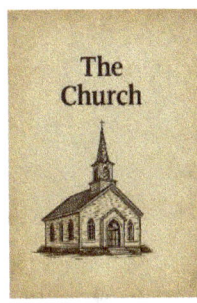

The Church

Pray for believers walking through difficult circumstances—that they would not lose heart but seek to understand God's greater purpose in their trials.

Pray that they would trust His wisdom, rest in His love, and allow the refining work of the Holy Spirit to shape them to be more like Christ through every challenge.

_____

_____

_____

_____

_____

_____

_____

_____

_____

_____

_____

_____

_____

_____

_____

_____

_____

_____

_____

The Great Commission

Pastors of small churches often face immense challenges that go unseen. With limited financial resources, small congregations, and often no staff support, these faithful shepherds carry a heavy burden. They are expected to wear many hats. The isolation can be overwhelming and discouraging, especially in a world that often equates success with size and visibility.

Ask God to refresh their spirits. Pray that they would experience God's presence and be strengthened.

_____

_____

_____

_____

_____

_____

_____

_____

_____

_____

_____

_____

_____

_____

_____

_____

Prayer for Others

Choose a young mother to pray for.

Ask the Holy Spirit to surround her with His presence and pour out abundant blessings over every area of her life.

Pray that God would give her supernatural strength for each day, and wisdom beyond her years to guide, nurture, and care for her family.

Ask the Lord to give her His peace when she feels overwhelmed, clarity when making decisions, and to provide her with strong godly mentors and friends.

Pray that her home would be filled with love, joy, and the presence of God.

_____

_____

_____

_____

_____

_____

_____

_____

_____

_____

_____

_____

_____

_____

Ask the Holy Spirit to fill you afresh and renew your spirit.

Invite Him to restore your joy, calm every anxious thought, and flood your heart with His perfect peace.

Declare boldly that the Lord is your refuge and strength, your ever-present help in times of need.

_____

_____

_____

_____

_____

_____

_____

_____

_____

_____

_____

_____

_____

_____

_____

_____

_____

_____

Weekly Scripture Focus

"Blessed be the Lord my Rock, who trains my hands for war, and my fingers for battle—

My lovingkindness and my fortress, My high tower and my deliverer, My shield and the One in whom I take refuge, Who subdues my people under me.

LORD, what is man, that You take knowledge of him? Or the son of man, that You are mindful of him?

Man is like a breath; His days are like a passing shadow.

Bow down Your heavens, O LORD, and come down; touch the mountains, and they shall smoke.

Flash forth lightning and scatter them; shoot out Your arrows and destroy them. Stretch out Your hand from above; rescue me and deliver me out of great waters, from the hand of foreigners.

Whose mouth speaks lying words, and whose right hand is a right hand of falsehood.

I will sing a new song to You, O God; on a harp of ten strings I will sing praises to You." Psalm 144:1-9

As your prayer begins this week, lift up praise to God for His recent provision, and repent of wrongdoing—praying on behalf of yourself, others, the Church, and your nation.

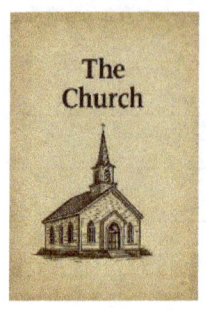

The Church

It is God's will that we be transformed into the image of His Son, Jesus Christ, and Satan opposes God's will. This transformation is a divine process that requires our cooperation. As believers, Satan tries to frustrate us, but God has equipped us—training our hands for spiritual battle—so that we can resist and overcome the enemy, who seeks to hinder this work of change in our lives.

Thank God for the provision He has made for us as the Church.

_____

_____

_____

_____

_____

_____

_____

_____

_____

_____

_____

_____

_____

_____

_____

_____

_____

_____

The Great Commission

"Therefore pray the Lord of the harvest to send out laborers into His harvest." Matthew 9:38

Ask God to prepare hearts to receive the Gospel, and to draw multitudes out of darkness and into the light of Christ.

Pray for a great awakening in communities, cities, and nations—that many would repent, believe, and be transformed by the power of God.

Prayer for Others

Pray for the neighbor next door.

Ask the Lord to open doors for meaningful connection and conversation.

Pray for divine appointments and opportunities to show Christ's love in practical ways.

Ask God to prepare their heart to receive the truth of the Gospel.

Pray for wisdom, and sensitivity as you interact with them.

Ask God to draw them into His kingdom and to use you as His vessel of light and love right where you live.

_____

_____

_____

_____

_____

_____

_____

_____

_____

_____

_____

_____

_____

_____

Bless the Lord for being your unshakable rock and firm foundation.

Praise Him for training your hands for spiritual battle and your fingers for warfare.

Thank Him that His unfailing love surrounds you like a mighty fortress, shielding and strengthening you in every trial.

_____

_____

_____

_____

_____

_____

_____

_____

_____

_____

_____

_____

_____

_____

_____

_____

_____

_____

Weekly Scripture Focus

"At that time Michael shall stand up, the great prince who stands watch over the sons of your people; And there shall be a time of trouble, such as never was since there was a nation, even to that time. And at that time your people shall be delivered, everyone who is found written in the book.

And many of those who sleep in the dust of the earth shall awake, some to everlasting life, some to shame and everlasting contempt.

Those who are wise shall shine like the brightness of the firmament, and those who turn many to righteousness like the stars forever and ever." Daniel 12:1-3

As your prayer begins this week, lift up praise to God for His recent provision, and repent of wrongdoing—praying on behalf of yourself, others, the Church, and your nation.

_____

_____

_____

_____

_____

_____

_____

_____

_____

_____

_____

_____

The Church

Pray that we would be protected from the deception and delusion that mark these last days, remaining grounded in the truth of God's Word.

Pray that we would live with a sense of urgency and readiness for the Lord's return, keeping our hearts pure and our eyes fixed on Him.

Pray that our lamps would be burning brightly—trimmed and filled with oil—and that we would carry an overflow of the Holy Spirit to sustain us through every season.

The Great Commission

Pray that the Lord would raise up willing and obedient laborers to go into His harvest field.

Ask God to stir our hearts to live missionally—right where we are and to the ends of the earth.

Intercede for missionaries and their families, that God would protect, strengthen, and provide for all their spiritual, emotional, and practical needs.

 **Prayer for Others**

Choose a church in your local town to lift up in prayer.

Ask the Lord to pour out His Spirit upon that congregation in a fresh and powerful way.

Pray that the leadership will walk in wisdom, humility, and unity, and that the people will be deeply rooted in the Word of God.

Intercede for their ministries to flourish, for many salvations and disciples to be made, and for the love of Christ to be evident in all they do.

Pray that they would bear much fruit—fruit that remains, and that they are a beacon of hope, truth, and light in the community.

_____

_____

_____

_____

_____

_____

_____

_____

_____

_____

_____

_____

_____

_____

Ask God to let His Word continually shape and transform your heart, aligning your thoughts, desires, and actions with His will.

Pray that, like Daniel, you would have wisdom and discernment to understand the times you are living in, and to respond with faith, boldness, and obedience.

_____

_____

_____

_____

_____

_____

_____

_____

_____

_____

_____

_____

_____

_____

_____

_____

_____

_____

"Therefore I say to you, whatever things you ask when you pray, believe that you receive them, and you will have them." Mark 11:4

"Thus says the LORD, the Holy One of Israel, and His Maker, ask Me of things to come concerning My sons, and concerning the work of My hands command you Me." Isaiah 45:11

As your prayer begins this week, lift up praise to God for His recent provision, and repent of wrongdoing—praying on behalf of yourself, others, the Church, and your nation.

_____

_____

_____

_____

_____

_____

_____

_____

_____

_____

_____

_____

_____

_____

_____

_____

_____

The Church

Ask God for spiritual discernment to recognize and avoid the snares of the enemy, walking wisely and staying anchored in truth. Ephesians 6:11; Proverbs 3:5–6

Ask the Holy Spirit to train and guide us, that we may be equipped as good soldiers of Christ—disciplined, alert, and ready for battle. 2 Timothy 2:3–4; Psalm 144:1

_____

_____

_____

_____

_____

_____

_____

_____

_____

_____

_____

_____

_____

_____

_____

_____

_____

_____

The Great Commission

Pray for the nations that don't know the God of the Bible. Ask the Lord to shine the light of His truth in places where spiritual darkness has long prevailed.

Pray that God would call many out of darkness into His marvelous light, breaking through centuries of tradition, deception, and spiritual blindness.

Ask the Holy Spirit to prepare hearts, raise up bold witnesses, and bring divine revelations of Jesus Christ through dreams, visions, and the testimony of believers.

Prayer for Others

Pray for the children born into nations and families who don't know the God of the Bible and have never heard the truth of the Gospel of Jesus Christ.

Pray that God would soften their hearts from a young age, protect them from indoctrination, and allow them to encounter the love of Christ.

Pray that the Word of God would reach them through online resources, Bible stories, or compassionate believers who cross their paths.

Pray that a new generation would rise up to follow Jesus, even in the face of persecution.

_____

_____

_____

_____

_____

_____

_____

_____

_____

_____

_____

_____

_____

_____

_____

Ask God to fill you with the knowledge of His Will.

To open the eyes of your understanding.

To give you spiritual wisdom and discernment.

Ask Him to help you know what pleases Him, to align your thoughts and actions with His purposes to walk in obedience to His Word. Surrender your plans to His will.

_____

_____

_____

_____

_____

_____

_____

_____

_____

_____

_____

_____

_____

_____

_____

_____

_____

Weekly Scripture Focus

"For we do not wrestle against flesh and blood, but against principalities, against powers, against the rulers of the darkness of this age, against spiritual hosts of wickedness in the heavenly places. Therefore take up the whole armor of God, that you may be able to withstand in the evil day, and having done all, to stand." Ephesians 6:12,13

Why is there antagonism against Christians, and why do we feel the need to prove we are right? How do we sidestep unnecessary battles with flesh and blood? How do we guard against the enemy's tactics that draw us into these skirmishes? Why must we have patience with people, and why must we show meekness, which is strength under control? Why does a soft answer turn away wrath?

Knowing that our battle is not against flesh and blood, it is sometimes better to walk away, and begin to do battle in prayer, as the weapons of our warfare are mighty to the pulling down of strongholds.

As your prayer begins this week, lift up praise to God for His recent provision, and repent of wrongdoing—praying on behalf of yourself, others, the Church, and your nation.

_____

_____

_____

_____

_____

_____

_____

The Church

Ask God to give us sharp spiritual discernment to recognize and avoid the subtle snares and deceptions of the enemy.

Pray that we would walk in wisdom, remain steadfast in truth, and be fully clothed in the armor of God. Pray that we would become strong soldiers of the Cross.

Pray that all our trust would be in God, that we would not lean on our own understanding, but that we will acknowledge Him in all our ways as He directs our paths." Proverbs 3:5-6

_____

_____

_____

_____

_____

_____

_____

_____

_____

_____

_____

_____

_____

_____

_____

_____

_____

The Great Commission

Pray for those imprisoned behind bars—especially those serving long or life sentences, with little or no hope of release.

Lift up those who have no family support because of bad decisions and they feel forgotten and abandoned.

Pray that the light of the Gospel would penetrate even the darkest prison cell.

Ask God to raise up prison chaplains, volunteers, and fellow inmates who know Christ to bring hope, comfort, and truth to transform their hearts and give them a new identity in Christ.

_____

_____

_____

_____

_____

_____

_____

_____

_____

_____

_____

_____

_____

_____

_____

_____

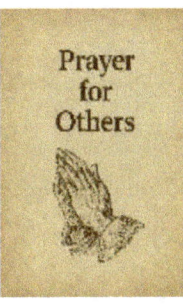

Prayer for Others

Pray for volunteers who will faithfully give their time and energy to serve in the Lord's work.

Ask God to strengthen and refresh them, so that they would not grow weary in well-doing.

Pray that they endure and would be encouraged knowing that their labor is not in vain.

Ask for provision for their needs and blessing for their families.

Pray that their service is not out of obligation, but out of a heart of love, and that they will find fulfillment and purpose in serving Christ.

_____

_____

_____

_____

_____

_____

_____

_____

_____

_____

_____

_____

_____

_____

_____

_____

_____

Ask God to place a new song of praise in your heart—one that flows from deep gratitude and love.

As you worship, sing it out to Him with joy and reverence, declaring His goodness and glory.

_____

_____

_____

_____

_____

_____

_____

_____

_____

_____

_____

_____

_____

_____

_____

_____

_____

_____

_____

_____

"And Moses said to the people, "Do not be afraid. Stand still, and see the salvation of the LORD, which He will accomplish for you today. For the Egyptians whom you see today, you shall see again no more forever. The LORD will fight for you, and you shall hold your peace." Exodus 14:13-14

Many believers deem the subject of spiritual warfare burdensome and pessimistic. They believe the Christian existence should be like a utopia, but the only paradise on earth is a false one. By refusing to engage in the fight, we remain immature and fail to become effective soldiers of the Lord Jesus, even decades after our conversion, often becoming casualties of war. We cannot enter the kingdom of God's dear Son without facing this struggle against the powers of darkness, and we cannot expect the enemy to give up easily. His aim is to harm or hinder us, take us prisoner, or destroy our faith completely; it is an ongoing struggle. Take courage that God is on our side.

As your prayer begins this week, lift up praise to God for His recent provision, and repent of wrongdoing—praying on behalf of yourself, others, the Church, and your nation.

_____

_____

_____

_____

_____

_____

_____

_____

The Church

Pray that believers would understand that God is for us, that He fights for us, and He walks through trials with us.

Pray that when we go through difficulties that we would not be afraid but be strong and stand still. God has never failed us, and He never will.

_____
_____
_____
_____
_____
_____
_____
_____
_____
_____
_____
_____
_____
_____
_____
_____
_____
_____
_____
_____

The Great Commission

Pray for the protection and safety of those who preach the Gospel in China and North Korea, Iran, and other hostile places.

Pray for favor, open doors, and signs and wonders to proceed with the preaching of the Gospel.

_____

_____

_____

_____

_____

_____

_____

_____

_____

_____

_____

_____

_____

_____

_____

_____

_____

_____

_____

_____

_____

Prayer for Others

Pray for the suffering children around the world—that God would raise up compassionate warriors to rescue, protect, and advocate for them.

Ask the Lord to bring healing, justice, and hope into their lives.

_____

_____

_____

_____

_____

_____

_____

_____

_____

_____

_____

_____

_____

_____

_____

_____

_____

_____

_____

_____

_____

Just as God brought the Israelites through the Red Sea, ask God to help you trust His plan. He loves you.

Pray that you will rest in His promises and watch as He brings deliverance and victory in His perfect way and time.

Believe God's Word and thank Him in advance.

Weekly Scripture Focus

"He said to them, But who do you say that I am?

Simon Peter answered and said, You are the Christ, the Son of the living God.

Jesus answered and said to him, 'Blessed are you, Simon Bar-Jonah, for flesh and blood has not revealed this to you, but My Father who is in heaven. And I also say to you that you are Peter, and on this rock, I will build My church, and the gates of Hades shall not prevail against it.'" Matthew 16:15-18

"He who has an ear, let him hear what the Spirit says to the churches." Revelation 3:22

As your prayer begins this week, lift up praise to God for His recent provision, and repent of wrongdoing—praying on behalf of yourself, others, the Church, and your nation.

_____

_____

_____

_____

_____

_____

_____

_____

_____

_____

_____

_____

_____

The Church

Pray that as believers, we would have ears to hear what the Spirit is saying to the Church in these last days, with hearts willing to respond in obedience and faith.

Pray for spiritual discernment and that we would clearly recognize God's voice. Ask the Holy Spirit to silence every distracting or insignificant voice trying to influence or mislead us.

Pray that we would live with a sense of urgency and readiness, keeping our lamps trimmed, and our hearts prepared for the return of the Lord.

_____

_____

_____

_____

_____

_____

_____

_____

_____

_____

_____

_____

_____

_____

_____

The Great Commission

Pray that when it comes to sharing the Gospel, we would speak the Word of God with boldness and declare that *"Therefore if the Son makes you free, you shall be free indeed."* John 8:36

Pray that the seed would fall on good ground and that we would see people drawn to the Light of God and the truth of His Word.

Pray for the peace of Jerusalem and the Jewish people to accept their Messiah.

_____

_____

_____

_____

_____

_____

_____

_____

_____

_____

_____

_____

_____

_____

_____

_____

_____

Prayer for Others

Pray for families dealing with addiction, that the Lord would set them free.

Pray against the feeling of hopelessness and desperation and declare: *"Jesus Christ is the same yesterday, today, and forever."* Hebrews 13:8

Nothing is impossible for Him. When He died on the cross and was resurrected from the grave, He destroyed the power of sin, evil, and death.

Pray that God would expose the root of the problem so that it can be dealt with.

_____

_____

_____

_____

_____

_____

_____

_____

_____

_____

_____

_____

_____

_____

_____

_____

Ask the Lord to deepen your compassion for those who are often overlooked or rejected by society—those who feel like misfits or who struggle to find their place.

Pray that He would open your heart, guide your steps, and show you how to be a true friend to them, reflecting His love and acceptance.

_____

_____

_____

_____

_____

_____

_____

_____

_____

_____

_____

_____

_____

_____

_____

_____

_____

Weekly Scripture Focus

The Dry Bones Live

"The hand of the Lord came upon me and brought me out in the Spirit of the Lord and set me down in the midst of the valley; and it was full of bones. Then He caused me to pass by them all around, and behold, there were very many in the open valley; and indeed, they were very dry. And He said to me, 'Son of man, can these bones live?'

So, I answered, 'O Lord God, You know.'

Again He said to me, 'Prophesy to these bones, and say to them, 'O dry bones, hear the word of the Lord!' Thus says the Lord God to these bones: 'Surely, I will cause breath to enter into you, and you shall live. I will put sinews on you and bring flesh upon you, cover you with skin and put breath in you; and you shall live. Then you shall know that I am the Lord.' So I prophesied as I was commanded; and as I prophesied, there was a noise, and suddenly a rattling; and the bones came together, bone to bone. Indeed, as I looked, the sinews and the flesh came upon them, and the skin covered them over; but there was no breath in them.

Also He said to me, 'Prophesy to the breath, prophesy, son of man, and say to the breath, 'Thus says the Lord God: Come from the four winds, O breath, and breathe on these slain, that they may live' So I prophesied as He commanded me, and breath came into them, and they lived, and stood upon their feet, an exceedingly great army. Then He said to me, 'Son of man, these bones are the whole house of Israel. They indeed say, 'Our bones are dry, our hope is lost, and we ourselves are cut off!' Therefore prophesy and say to them, 'Thus says the Lord God: 'Behold, O My people, I will open your graves and cause you to come up from your graves and bring you into the land of Israel. Then you shall know that I am the Lord, when I have opened your graves, O My people, and brought you up from your graves. I will put My Spirit in you, and you shall live, and I will place you in your own land. Then

you shall know that I, the Lord, have spoken it and performed it,' says the Lord."
Ezekiel 37:1-14

As your prayer begins this week, lift up praise to God for His recent provision, and repent of wrongdoing—praying on behalf of yourself, others, the Church, and your nation.

_____

_____

_____

_____

_____

_____

_____

_____

_____

_____

_____

_____

_____

_____

_____

_____

_____

_____

_____

_____

The Church

Pray for an outpouring of the Holy Spirit on the church, that we would be connected to one another, and that the Holy Spirit would breathe new life into our churches.

The Great Commission

Pray that revival would sweep across our nation—awakening hearts with deep Holy Spirit conviction, leading to true repentance and a great harvest of souls.

Ask the Lord to start this work within all of us, renewing our hearts and filling us with His fire.

Prayer for Others

Pray for families—fathers, mothers, children, grandchildren, and extended relatives.

Ask God to bring salvation to entire households and draw every family member into a living relationship with Jesus.

Pray that He would establish them in His Church, rooted in truth and love, growing together in faith and purpose.

Surrender every burden you carry to the Lord, laying them at His feet in faith. Boldly declare, *"For with God nothing will be impossible."* Luke 1:37. Trust that He is working on your behalf—even in ways beyond your understanding. Thank Him in advance for the answers, believing that His timing and methods are perfect.

_____

_____

_____

_____

_____

_____

_____

_____

_____

_____

_____

_____

_____

_____

_____

_____

_____

_____

Weekly Scripture Focus

"God has spoken once, Twice I have heard this: That power belongs to God. Also to You, O Lord, belongs mercy; For You render to each one according to his work." Psalm 62:11-12

"But Jesus looked at them and said to them, 'With men this is impossible, but with God all things are possible.'" (Matthew 19:26)

As your prayer begins this week, lift up praise to God for His recent provision, and repent of wrongdoing—praying on behalf of yourself, others, the Church, and your nation.

_____

_____

_____

_____

_____

_____

_____

_____

_____

_____

_____

_____

_____

_____

_____

_____

_____

_____

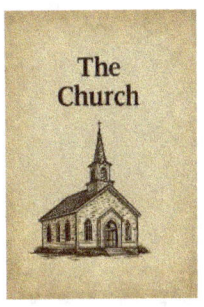

The Church

Pray that we would grow in the grace and knowledge of our Lord Jesus Christ—deepening our relationship with Him through His Word and Spirit.

Ask that we may comprehend the height, breadth, length, and depth of God's love, and live securely in it.

Pray that our minds would be continually renewed and transformed, aligning with His truth, so that we may walk in wisdom, faith, and spiritual maturity.

_____

_____

_____

_____

_____

_____

_____

_____

_____

_____

_____

_____

_____

_____

_____

_____

_____

The Great Commission

"Therefore pray the Lord of the harvest to send out laborers into His harvest." Matthew 9: 38

Pray that as the Gospel is proclaimed, it will break through demonic resistance and break the strongholds of evil in people's lives.

Ask God to encourage those laboring in the harvest field, as they witness lives transformed and people set free.

Prayer for Others

Ask the Holy Spirit to give you a prophetic word of encouragement for a friend—something timely, Spirit-led, and full of grace.

Pray that the Lord blesses them with His perfect peace and that His Word to them would bring comfort, strength, and direction. Declare:

"A word fitly spoken is like apples of gold in settings of silver." Proverbs 25:11

Ask God to make your words beautifully timely and deeply impactful.

_____

_____

_____

_____

_____

_____

_____

_____

_____

_____

_____

_____

_____

_____

_____

_____

_____

_____

Thank God for all His many blessings He has bestowed on you.

Thank Him for the good friends you have, especially those who keep you accountable.

Thank Him for His protection and provision.

Weekly Scripture Focus

"Beloved, now we are children of God; and it has not yet been revealed what we shall be, but we know that when He is revealed, we shall be like Him, for we shall see Him as He is. And everyone who has this hope in Him purifies himself, just as He is pure." 1 John 3:2-3

"I must work the works of Him who sent Me while it is day; the night is coming when no one can work. As long as I am in the world, I am the light of the world." John 9:4

"There is no fear in love; but perfect love casts out fear, because fear involves torment. But he who fears has not been made perfect in love." 1 John 4:18

Why is it important to prepare for the coming of the Lord? Why should we be busy working for the Lord while we still have time and not be afraid of man?

As your prayer begins this week, lift up praise to God for His recent provision, and repent of wrongdoing—praying on behalf of yourself, others, the Church, and your nation.

_____

_____

_____

_____

_____

_____

_____

_____

_____

The Church

Ask the Holy Spirit to help us redeem the time and make the most of every opportunity as we labor faithfully for the Lord.

Pray that each one of us would live with purpose, urgency, and sensitivity to His leading, using our time wisely. Jesus will be returning soon.

The Great Commission

Pray that the Gospel would penetrate unreachable regions of the world with power and truth.

Ask that Jesus would reveal Himself through visions and dreams to those living in spiritual darkness.

Pray that the Holy Spirit would draw them out of deception and lead them into the light and truth of Christ.

Prayer for Others

Pray for those who are grieving the loss of loved ones.

Ask the Lord to surround them with His comforting presence, to carry them through waves of sorrow, and to give them strength for each new day.

Pray that they would not feel alone, but would sense the nearness of God, who is close to the brokenhearted.

Ask the Holy Spirit to bring peace to their minds, healing to their broken hearts, and the hope of resurrection when Jesus returns.

_____

_____

_____

_____

_____

_____

_____

_____

_____

_____

_____

_____

_____

_____

_____

_____

_____

Jesus is coming soon; may you understand the urgency of the time.

Pray for wisdom to use every moment for His glory— there is no time to waste.

Let your light shine wherever you go.

_____

_____

_____

_____

_____

_____

_____

_____

_____

_____

_____

_____

_____

_____

_____

_____

_____

"Therefore prepare yourself and arise, and speak to them all that I command you. Do not be dismayed before their faces, lest I dismay you before them." Jeremiah 1:17

"The Spirit of the LORD is upon Me, because He has anointed Me to preach the gospel to the poor; He has sent Me to heal the brokenhearted, to proclaim liberty to the captives and recovery of sight to the blind, to set at liberty those who are oppressed." Luke 4:18

As your prayer begins this week, lift up praise to God for His recent provision, and repent of wrongdoing—praying on behalf of yourself, others, the Church, and your nation.

_____

_____

_____

_____

_____

_____

_____

_____

_____

_____

_____

_____

_____

_____

_____

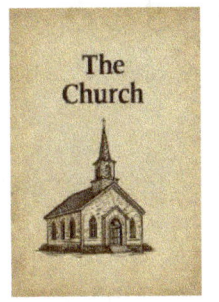

The Church

Pray that as believers we would be effective in God's Kingdom. We have been set apart and anointed by God and have been given a ministry of reconciliation.

Pray that we would understand our calling to help others come into the kingdom.

Pray for those who are struggling to stand. Walk alongside them and encourage them.

The Great Commission

Pray that the Spirit of the Lord would rest upon us as we witness, empowering us with boldness and compassion.

Ask that broken hearts be healed, the lame walk, the deaf hear, and the blind receive sight.

Pray that those held in bondage—spiritually, emotionally, or physically— be set free by the power of Jesus.

_____

_____

_____

_____

_____

_____

_____

_____

_____

_____

_____

_____

_____

_____

_____

_____

_____

_____

Prayer for Others

Choose a family—whether your own or another close to your heart—and lift each member before the Lord by name.

Pray that God would surround them with His presence, meet their individual and collective needs, and strengthen their relationships.

Ask for healing where there is brokenness, provision where there is lack, and guidance in every decision they face.

Pray for peace to reign in their home, and for each person to walk in God's purpose for their life.

_____

_____

_____

_____

_____

_____

_____

_____

_____

_____

_____

_____

_____

_____

_____

_____

Ask God to make this week fruitful —in your work, relationships, and spiritual walk.

Pray for divine opportunities, open doors, and wisdom to walk in His will.

Take time to praise Him with a thankful heart for all the good things He has done, and for his faithfulness to you.

_____
_____
_____
_____
_____
_____
_____
_____
_____
_____
_____
_____
_____
_____
_____
_____
_____
_____

<table>
<tr><td>

Weekly Scripture Focus

</td><td>

"But Jesus said, 'Let the little children come to Me, and do not forbid them; for of such is the kingdom of heaven.'" Matthew 19:14

</td></tr>
</table>

What is happening to children all over the world? Why does Satan target them? How does God see children? What's our responsibility in prayer?

As your prayer begins this week, lift up praise to God for His recent provision, and repent of wrongdoing—praying on behalf of yourself, others, the Church, and your nation.

_____

_____

_____

_____

_____

_____

_____

_____

_____

_____

_____

_____

_____

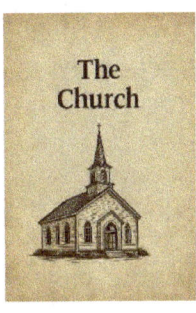

The Church

Ask God to give parents wisdom, strength, and discernment to protect their children from ungodly influences and to cultivate an environment where faith, integrity, and love for God can flourish.

Pray for the Children's Ministry in the Church, that they would communicate the Gospel to the children with clarity.

The Great Commission

Pray that the unevangelized would receive a divine revelation of Jesus Christ as the Son of God and the Redeemer of the world.

Ask that the Gospel would go forth with supernatural power—confirming signs, miracles, and transformed lives—as undeniable evidence of its truth, drawing hearts to repentance and salvation.

_____

_____

_____

_____

_____

_____

_____

_____

_____

_____

_____

_____

_____

_____

_____

_____

_____

_____

_____

Prayer for Others

Choose a child to pray for.

Ask the Lord to give you a specific promise from His Word to declare over their life.

Pray that this promise will take root in their heart, guide their steps, and shape their future.

_____

_____

_____

_____

_____

_____

_____

_____

_____

_____

_____

_____

_____

_____

_____

_____

_____

_____

_____

_____

Ask God to give you simple, unwavering childlike faith—and a heart that trusts Him completely, without fear or doubt, in every circumstance. Thank Him for hearing your prayer.

_____

_____

_____

_____

_____

_____

_____

_____

_____

_____

_____

_____

_____

_____

_____

_____

_____

_____

_____

Weekly Scripture Focus

"Then the disciples came to Jesus privately and said, 'Why could we not cast it out?' So Jesus said to them, 'Because of your unbelief; for assuredly, I say to you, if you have faith as a mustard seed, you will say to this mountain, 'Move from here to there,' and it will move; and nothing will be impossible for you. However, this kind does not go out except by prayer and fasting.'" Matthew 17:19-21

"So those who fed the swine fled, and they told it in the city and in the country. And they went out to see what it was that had happened. Then they came to Jesus and saw the one who had been demon-possessed and had the legion, sitting and clothed and in his right mind. And they were afraid. And those who saw it told them how it happened to him who had been demon-possessed, and about the swine." Mark 5:14-16

Jesus has so much compassion for the demon possessed, He casts out the demons and sets the people free. Why does unbelief hinder us from doing what Jesus did?

As your prayer begins this week, lift up praise to God for His recent provision, and repent of wrongdoing—praying on behalf of yourself, others, the Church, and your nation.

_____

_____

_____

_____

_____

_____

_____

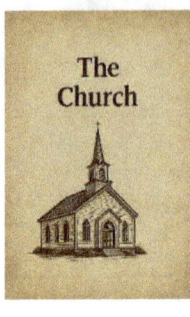

The Church

Pray that God would break the stronghold of unbelief in our hearts and minds.

Ask the Holy Spirit to increase our faith. Pray that we would trust God's Word fully, and believe His promises even when circumstances seem contrary. Mark 9:24, Hebrews 11:6

_____

_____

_____

_____

_____

_____

_____

_____

_____

_____

_____

_____

_____

_____

_____

_____

_____

_____

_____

The Great Commission

Make this declaration:

"And these signs will follow those who believe: In My name they will cast out demons; they will speak with new tongues." Mark 16:17

Pray that as the Gospel is preached, the power of God would be made manifest—bringing deliverance to the oppressed, healing to the broken, and freedom to those bound by darkness.

Ask that signs and wonders would confirm the Word, and that many would be set free in Jesus' name.

_____

_____

_____

_____

_____

_____

_____

_____

_____

_____

_____

_____

_____

_____

_____

_____

_____

Prayer for Others

Pray for your mother and father, if they are still in your life.

Ask God to bless them and meet their every need—whether physical, emotional, or spiritual.

If they do not yet know Jesus, pray that God would soften their hearts and give you the opportunity and grace to lovingly introduce them to the Savior.

_____

_____

_____

_____

_____

_____

_____

_____

_____

_____

_____

_____

_____

_____

_____

_____

_____

_____

Ask the Holy Spirit to breathe fresh life into your walk with Christ—renewing your passion, deepening your hunger for God's presence, and restoring joy, purpose, and spiritual vitality.

_____

_____

_____

_____

_____

_____

_____

_____

_____

_____

_____

_____

_____

_____

_____

_____

_____

_____

Weekly Scripture Focus

"When the Day of Pentecost had fully come, they were all with one accord in one place. And suddenly there came a sound from heaven, as of a rushing mighty wind, and it filled the whole house where they were sitting. Then there appeared to them divided tongues, as of fire, and one sat upon each of them. And they were all filled with the Holy Spirit and began to speak with other tongues, as the Spirit gave them utterance." Acts 2:1-4

As your prayer begins this week, lift up praise to God for His recent provision, and repent of wrongdoing—praying on behalf of yourself, others, the Church, and your nation.

_____

_____

_____

_____

_____

_____

_____

_____

_____

_____

_____

_____

_____

_____

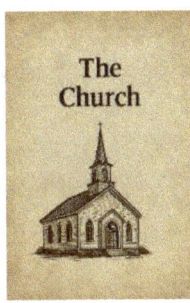

The Church

Pray that new believers will receive the baptism of the Holy Spirit.

Pray that they can grow and flourish in their walk with Christ.

Pray that evidence of the power that they received is a bold witness.

Ask God to surround them with His protection and to strengthen their faith.

_____

_____

_____

_____

_____

_____

_____

_____

_____

_____

_____

_____

_____

_____

_____

_____

_____

_____

The Great Commission

Pray that as the Gospel is preached by those God has sent, it will result in chains breaking and hearts being set free by the power of Jesus Christ.

Ask the Lord for authority and power over attempts of the enemy to stop people from responding to the Gospel—bringing a mighty harvest of souls.

Pray for the conviction of the Holy Spirit bringing people to repentance, and that they would receive the free gift of salvation, and experience true transformation and new life.

_____

_____

_____

_____

_____

_____

_____

_____

_____

_____

_____

_____

_____

_____

_____

_____

Prayer for Others

Choose a new believer to pray for this week.

Ask God to protect the Word that has been sown in their heart.

Pray that the enemy would not steal it, that it would not be choked by the cares of this world or trampled underfoot, but that their heart would be fertile soil—open, nourished, and ready to receive all that God desires to do in them.

Pray that the seed would take deep root, grow strong, and bear lasting fruit.

_____

_____

_____

_____

_____

_____

_____

_____

_____

_____

_____

_____

_____

_____

_____

_____

_____

Pray that God would fill you with boldness to share the Gospel without fear.

Ask the Holy Spirit to open doors of opportunity, and to prepare the hearts of those you will speak to, so they may receive the truth with joy.

_____

_____

_____

_____

_____

_____

_____

_____

_____

_____

_____

_____

_____

_____

_____

_____

_____

_____

Weekly Scripture Focus

"Praise the LORD, call upon His name; declare His deeds among the peoples, make mention that His name is exalted.

Sing to the LORD, for He has done excellent things; this is known in all the earth." Isaiah 12:4-5

Read Psalm 149.

Why is it good to praise and give thanks for answered prayer?

As your prayer begins this week, lift up praise to God for His recent provision, and repent of wrongdoing—praying on behalf of yourself, others, the Church, and your nation.

_____

_____

_____

_____

_____

_____

_____

_____

_____

_____

_____

_____

_____

_____

_____

_____

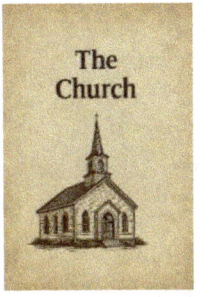

The Church

Pray for healing for those who are sick.

Pray for those who are struggling with addictions. Ask God to set them free.

Pray against anxiety and depression that takes believers into bondage. Ask God to give them peace.

Pray for those who have grown cold, and ask God to draw them back.

_____

_____

_____

_____

_____

_____

_____

_____

_____

_____

_____

_____

_____

_____

_____

_____

_____

_____

The Great Commission

Stand in the gap for those on the front lines of God's work.

Pray for pastors to remain steadfast and uncompromising in preaching the truth. Intercede for Children's Church workers, that they would clearly and creatively communicate the Gospel in a way that even the youngest hearts can understand. Lift up those ministering to teenagers, that they may be equipped with wisdom and grace to guide youth through moral challenges, social pressures, and identity struggles.

_____

_____

_____

_____

_____

_____

_____

_____

_____

_____

_____

_____

_____

_____

_____

_____

_____

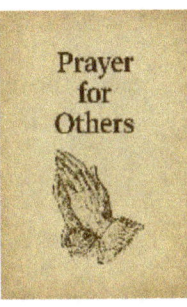

Prayer for Others

Pray for those who are shut-in and unable to gather with their church family.

Ask God to comfort them in their loneliness and surround them with His presence.

If you know someone in this situation, reach out with love, encouragement, or practical help.

If you're unable to do so, ask the Lord to send a caring worker into their lives—a messenger of hope and fellowship.

_____

_____

_____

_____

_____

_____

_____

_____

_____

_____

_____

_____

_____

_____

_____

_____

_____

Praise silences the enemy—he trembles before those who lift high the name of the Lord, even in the midst of trials.

Declare the greatness of God in every circumstance, knowing that worship is a weapon.

Spend time in His presence and praise Him, not only for what He has done, but for what He is doing and will yet do. Let your praise be a bold declaration of trust and victory in Christ.

Weekly Scripture Focus

"But if you are led by the Spirit, you are not under the law." Galatians 5:18

"That you may walk worthy of the Lord, fully pleasing Him, being fruitful in every good work and increasing in the knowledge of God." Colossians 1:10

As your prayer begins this week, lift up praise to God for His recent provision, and repent of wrongdoing—praying on behalf of yourself, others, the Church, and your nation.

_____

_____

_____

_____

_____

_____

_____

_____

_____

_____

_____

_____

_____

_____

_____

_____

The Church

Pray that we would be led by the Holy Spirit in all things, walking in step with Him.

Pray for a spirit of unity among believers—one heart and one mind in Christ.

Ask that we grow continually in the knowledge of God, deepening our understanding of His Word, His will, and His ways.

_____

_____

_____

_____

_____

_____

_____

_____

_____

_____

_____

_____

_____

_____

_____

_____

_____

_____

_____

_____

_____

The Great Commission

Then He said to His disciples: *"The harvest truly is plentiful, but the laborers are few. Therefore pray the Lord of the harvest to send out laborers into His harvest."* Matthew 9:37-38—God wants faithful, Spirit-filled men and women ready to reap the souls ripe for salvation.

Intercede for the multitudes still in the "Valley of Decision," and for those under spiritual attack, harassed by the enemy who roams like a roaring lion seeking whom he may devour.

Ask God to raise up bold witnesses who carry His power, compassion, and truth to rescue the lost.

 **Prayer for Others**

If you know a missionary, lift them up in prayer today.

Ask God to increase their fruitfulness, strengthen their spirit, and pour out a fresh anointing upon their life and ministry. If possible, encourage them—send a message, write a letter, let them know you're praying for them.

A word of support can refresh the heart of a faithful servant in the field.

_____

_____

_____

_____

_____

_____

_____

_____

_____

_____

_____

_____

_____

_____

_____

_____

_____

Ask God to open your spiritual eyes to see His Kingdom and your ears to hear His voice clearly.

Invite the Holy Spirit to search your heart and remove anything that hinders your walk with Him.

Pray that you may live a life worthy of your calling—fully pleasing to Him, bearing fruit in every good work, and growing in the knowledge of God.

Weekly Scripture Focus

"For you were once darkness, but now you are light in the Lord. Walk as children of light." Ephesians 5:8

How can we be salt and light?

As your prayer begins this week, lift up praise to God for His recent provision, and repent of wrongdoing—praying on behalf of yourself, others, the Church, and your nation.

_____

_____

_____

_____

_____

_____

_____

_____

_____

_____

_____

_____

_____

_____

_____

_____

_____

The Church

Pray that we would live with urgency and spiritual alertness, keeping our hearts pure and our lamps burning brightly, ready and watching for the Lord's return.

Pray that as the Word is preached it would shine light on the things that must change, and that the salt of God's Word will purify our hearts.

_____

_____

_____

_____

_____

_____

_____

_____

_____

_____

_____

_____

_____

_____

_____

_____

_____

_____

_____

_____

The Great Commission

Ask God to make you deeply missional in heart and lifestyle. Remember, Jesus is the Light of the World—and you are called to carry His light into every place of darkness.

Pray that His light will shine brightly through your words, actions, and presence, drawing others to Him wherever you go.

Prayer for Others

If you know someone walking in spiritual darkness:

Pray that the light of Christ would break through every stronghold, illuminate their heart with truth, and bring freedom and transformation by the power of the Holy Spirit.

_____

_____

_____

_____

_____

_____

_____

_____

_____

_____

_____

_____

_____

_____

_____

_____

_____

_____

_____

_____

Ask the Holy Spirit to make you a flaming torch in His hand—burning brightly with His presence—so that you may lead many out of darkness and into the glorious light of Christ.

_____

_____

_____

_____

_____

_____

_____

_____

_____

_____

_____

_____

_____

_____

_____

_____

_____

_____

 **Weekly Scripture Focus**

"Therefore I also, after I heard of your faith in the Lord Jesus and your love for all the saints, do not cease to give thanks for you, making mention of you in my prayers: that the God of our Lord Jesus Christ, the Father of glory, may give to you the spirit of wisdom and revelation in the knowledge of Him, the eyes of your understanding being enlightened; that you may know what is the hope of His calling, what are the riches of the glory of His inheritance in the saints, and what is the exceeding greatness of His power toward us who believe, according to the working of His mighty power which He worked in Christ when He raised Him from the dead and seated Him at His right hand in the heavenly places, far above all principality and power and might and dominion, and every name that is named, not only in this age but also in that which is to come." Ephesians 1:15-21

As your prayer begins this week, lift up praise to God for His recent provision, and repent of wrongdoing—praying on behalf of yourself, others, the Church, and your nation.

_____

_____

_____

_____

_____

_____

_____

_____

_____

The Church

Pray that pastors and spiritual leaders will remain steadfast in their commitment to the truth of God's Word, and that they will shepherd the people in their care with love.

Ask the Lord to grant them divine wisdom, deep understanding of Scripture, and the courage to lead His people with integrity, humility, and boldness—guided by the Holy Spirit in all they do.

_____

_____

_____

_____

_____

_____

_____

_____

_____

_____

_____

_____

_____

_____

_____

_____

_____

_____

The Great Commission

Pray for small churches and the pastors who labor faithfully, shepherding their congregations.

Ask the Holy Spirit to strengthen, refresh, and encourage them to stand firm in their calling no matter how difficult.

Pray that they would not grow weary in well-doing but continue steadfastly in the good work God has entrusted to them.

_____

_____

_____

_____

_____

_____

_____

_____

_____

_____

_____

_____

_____

_____

_____

_____

_____

Prayer for Others

If you know a schoolteacher pray for them this week.

Ask God to give them boldness, wisdom, and discernment.

Pray that they would resist the pressures of ungodly ideologies seeking to influence our children.

Ask the Holy Spirit to strengthen them to uphold righteousness and bring light as they strive to impact young lives.

Give them both grace and courage.

Ask the Holy Spirit to align your hopes, dreams, and aspirations with God's perfect will and His thoughts toward you. Surrender your plans to Him, trusting that His ways are higher, and His timing is perfect.

Give thanks that His plans for your life are full of hope, purpose, and peace. Jeremiah 29:11.

Weekly
Scripture
Focus

"That you do not become sluggish, but imitate those who through faith and patience inherit the promises." Hebrews 6:12

"That I may know Him and the power of His resurrection, and the fellowship of His sufferings, being conformed to His death." Philippians 3:10

How do we persevere while waiting for God to answer our prayers? Is it possible to have a heart of thanksgiving when we face difficulties?

As your prayer begins this week, lift up praise to God for His recent provision, and repent of wrongdoing—praying on behalf of yourself, others, the Church, and your nation.

_____

_____

_____

_____

_____

_____

_____

_____

_____

_____

_____

_____

_____

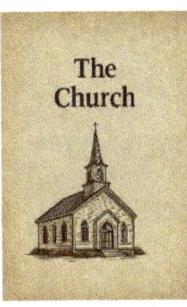

The Church

Pray that a spirit of praise would arise among us whenever we gather as the Church—that our hearts would overflow with thanksgiving, and we would bless the Lord for all He has done.

Prayer that our corporate worship will honor Him and create a dwelling place for His presence.

_____

_____

_____

_____

_____

_____

_____

_____

_____

_____

_____

_____

_____

_____

_____

_____

_____

_____

The Great Commission

Pray for those who are suffering or imprisoned for the sake of the Gospel.

Ask God to strengthen them with endurance, courage, and unshakable faith.

Lift up their families— pray that the Lord would provide for every need, surround them with His peace, and that the Holy Spirit would comfort and encourage them daily.

_____

_____

_____

_____

_____

_____

_____

_____

_____

_____

_____

_____

_____

_____

_____

_____

_____

_____

Prayer for Others

The Apostle Paul asked the Church to pray for him—and today, our spiritual leaders need our prayers just as much. They carry the weighty responsibility of guiding us in the things of God and will one day give an account for the souls entrusted to their care.

Pray that God would strengthen, protect, and lead them with wisdom, boldness, and humility as they shepherd His people.

_____

_____

_____

_____

_____

_____

_____

_____

_____

_____

_____

_____

_____

_____

_____

_____

_____

_____

_____

_____

_____

Ask God to increase His grace in your life. We are all called to grow in the grace and knowledge of the Lord, and when burdens feel heavy, He offers more grace.

Pray for a fresh outpouring of His grace so you can carry the burden of His heart with compassion, walk in His strength, and serve more effectively in your calling.

_____

_____

_____

_____

_____

_____

_____

_____

_____

_____

_____

_____

_____

_____

_____

_____

_____

Weekly Scripture Focus

"God is Spirit, and those who worship Him must worship in spirit and truth." John 4:24

"For I have come down from heaven, not to do My own will, but the will of Him who sent Me." John 6:38

His whole life was devoted to obeying His Father; yet it was not always easy for him. He was tempted in all ways as we are.

The definition of true worship is total surrender of your will to God and total obedience to His Word.

As your prayer begins this week, lift up praise to God for His recent provision, and repent of wrongdoing—praying on behalf of yourself, others, the Church, and your nation.

_____

_____

_____

_____

_____

_____

_____

_____

_____

_____

_____

_____

The Church

Pray that God's will be done on earth as it is in Heaven.

Pray that we, as believers, would fully align our lives with His purposes, turn away from everything that opposes His will, and walk in complete obedience and surrender.

_____
_____
_____
_____
_____
_____
_____
_____
_____
_____
_____
_____
_____
_____
_____
_____
_____
_____
_____
_____

The Great Commission

Pray that every scheme of the enemy to hinder the preaching of the Word in the world would be intercepted and dismantled by the power of the Holy Spirit.

Pray that as the Gospel is proclaimed, there would be freedom, divine favor, and an open heaven—so that hearts are receptive, and lives are transformed.

Declare the truth that God's Word never returns void, but accomplishes all He intends to do, as it goes forth in power.

_____

_____

_____

_____

_____

_____

_____

_____

_____

_____

_____

_____

_____

_____

_____

_____

Prayer for Others

Pray for a loved one who does not yet know Jesus as Lord.

Ask God to remove the veil that blinds their spiritual eyes, to soften their heart, and open their ears to hear His voice.

Pray that the Holy Spirit would reveal the truth of the Gospel to them in a deeply personal way, drawing them with His love, convicting them of truth, and leading them into a saving knowledge of Jesus Christ.

Declare that no plan of the enemy will hinder their salvation, and that God's light will shine into their darkness and transform their lives.

_____

_____

_____

_____

_____

_____

_____

_____

_____

_____

_____

_____

_____

_____

_____

"Lord, here I am—use me this week. Open my eyes to see the opportunities You place before me. Let my words, actions, and presence reflect Your love. Whether in big ways or small, help me to be Your hands and feet. Send me where I'm needed, and fill me with boldness, compassion, and wisdom to serve and glorify You."

_____

_____

_____

_____

_____

_____

_____

_____

_____

_____

_____

_____

_____

_____

_____

_____

_____

_____

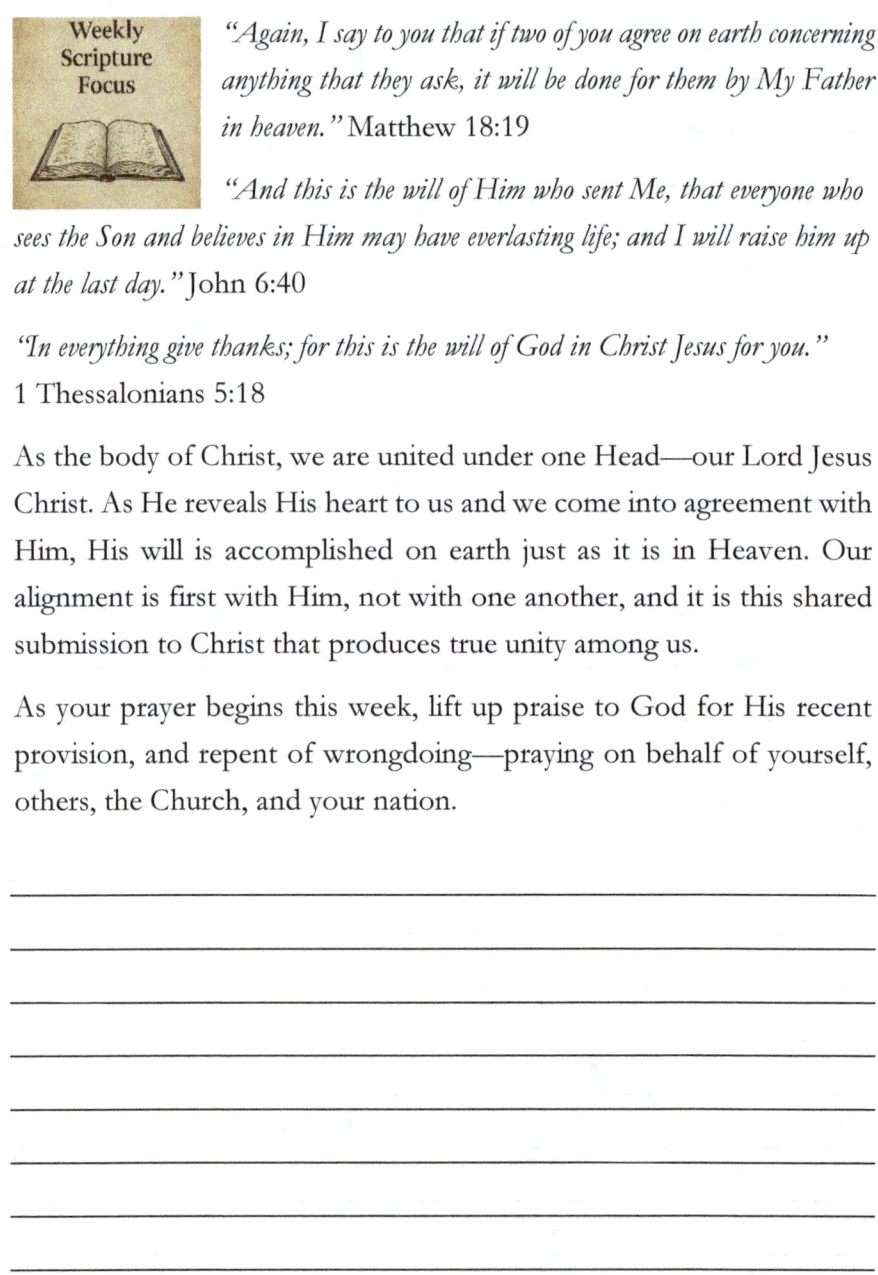

Weekly Scripture Focus

"Again, I say to you that if two of you agree on earth concerning anything that they ask, it will be done for them by My Father in heaven." Matthew 18:19

"And this is the will of Him who sent Me, that everyone who sees the Son and believes in Him may have everlasting life; and I will raise him up at the last day." John 6:40

"In everything give thanks; for this is the will of God in Christ Jesus for you." 1 Thessalonians 5:18

As the body of Christ, we are united under one Head—our Lord Jesus Christ. As He reveals His heart to us and we come into agreement with Him, His will is accomplished on earth just as it is in Heaven. Our alignment is first with Him, not with one another, and it is this shared submission to Christ that produces true unity among us.

As your prayer begins this week, lift up praise to God for His recent provision, and repent of wrongdoing—praying on behalf of yourself, others, the Church, and your nation.

_____

_____

_____

_____

_____

_____

_____

_____

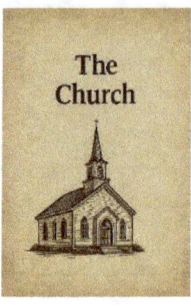

The Church

Pray that Jesus would be given pre-eminence in our church—that He would be exalted above all.

Pray that God alone would receive all the glory, and that the Holy Spirit would lead, guide, and have full control in all that we do.

_____

_____

_____

_____

_____

_____

_____

_____

_____

_____

_____

_____

_____

_____

_____

_____

_____

_____

_____

_____

The Great Commission

Pray for Sunday church services across the nation and around the world.

Ask that the presence of God would be tangible in every gathering, and that hearts would be open to the Gospel.

Pray that many would respond in faith, receive the free gift of eternal life through Jesus Christ, and be set free from every bondage. May there be a mighty harvest of souls and lasting transformation.

Prayer for Others

Pray for those who have experienced trauma—that God would bring deep healing to their minds, restore their peace, and renew their hope.

Ask the Lord to surround them with His presence and minister to every place of pain with His perfect love.

_____

_____

_____

_____

_____

_____

_____

_____

_____

_____

_____

_____

_____

_____

_____

_____

_____

_____

_____

Ask God to help you overcome every insecurity, fear, and limiting mindset that holds you back.

Pray for the courage, confidence, and faith to step fully into the calling and purpose He has prepared for your life.

Weekly Scripture Focus

"He has delivered us from the power of darkness and conveyed us into the kingdom of the Son of His love." Colossians 1:13

There are only two kingdoms, and they have nothing in common. There is nothing good in darkness, and nothing evil in God's light. The kingdom of darkness opposes the kingdom of light, but God shines His light into darkness and exposes it, and Jesus destroys the works of darkness, and rescues us out of the enemy's kingdom, changing our destiny.

In addition, Paul says that we are not only delivered, but God transforms us into new creations, and we become sons and daughters of God. We are not merely protected from the penalty of sin, but God removes it, and this is His will for everyone. What are the works of the enemy?

Why is the Gospel considered to be dynamite?

As your prayer begins this week, lift up praise to God for His recent provision, and repent of wrongdoing—praying on behalf of yourself, others, the Church, and your nation.

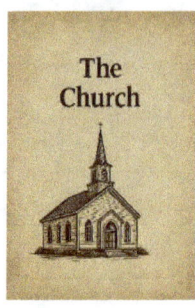

The Church

Pray that as believers, we would be bold and unashamed in our witness for Christ—living in such a way that our lives will reflect His light.

Pray that we would have no part in the unfruitful works of darkness but rather expose them by living in truth and righteousness, so that our testimony remains pure and powerful. Ephesians 5:11

_____

_____

_____

_____

_____

_____

_____

_____

_____

_____

_____

_____

_____

_____

_____

_____

_____

_____

The Great Commission

Pray for Strategic Missions and Church Planters:

Ask God to give them divine wisdom and strategies to reach the unreached.

Pray for supernatural help in learning local languages, favor with the communities they serve, and lasting fruit that remains for God's glory.

Pray earnestly for the peace of Jerusalem.

Ask the Holy Spirit to grant insight on how to intercede effectively.

_____

_____

_____

_____

_____

_____

_____

_____

_____

_____

_____

_____

_____

_____

_____

_____

Prayer for Others

Pray that the leaders in our community would come to know Jesus and govern with a deep sense of accountability before God and man, that they would walk in honesty, moral uprightness, and courage, not swayed by personal gain or hidden agendas.

Pray that the fear of the Lord would guide their decisions, and their leadership would be marked by transparency, truth, and righteousness.

Pray that God would expose and dismantle corruption and raise up trustworthy leaders who reflect His character and justice.

_____

_____

_____

_____

_____

_____

_____

_____

_____

_____

_____

_____

_____

_____

_____

_____

Take time to enter God's presence with thanksgiving, praise, and heartfelt worship.

Thank Him for who He is and for all He has done.

Let your heart overflow with gratitude as you exalt His name—because praise shifts the atmosphere, silences the enemy, and draws you closer to His heart.

_____

_____

_____

_____

_____

_____

_____

_____

_____

_____

_____

_____

_____

_____

_____

_____

_____

_____

Weekly Scripture Focus

"What then shall we say to these things? If God is for us, who can be against us? He who did not spare His own Son, but delivered Him up for us all, how shall He not with Him also freely give us all things? Who shall bring a charge against God's elect? It is God who justifies. Who is he who condemns? It is Christ who died, and furthermore is also risen, who is even at the right hand of God, who also makes intercession for us. Who shall separate us from the love of Christ? Shall tribulation, or distress, or persecution, or famine, or nakedness, or peril, or sword? As it is written:

'For Your sake we are killed all day long; We are accounted as sheep for the slaughter.'

Yet in all these things we are more than conquerors through Him who loved us. For I am persuaded that neither death nor life, nor angels nor principalities nor powers, nor things present nor things to come, nor height nor depth, nor any other created thing, shall be able to separate us from the love of God which is in Christ Jesus our Lord." Romans 8:31-39

As your prayer begins this week, lift up praise to God for His recent provision, and repent of wrongdoing—praying on behalf of yourself, others, the Church, and your nation.

_____

_____

_____

_____

_____

_____

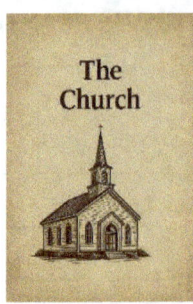

The Church

Pray that as believers, we would deeply understand that God is for us, and that nothing—no trial, no failure, no force—can separate us from His unfailing love. Romans 8:31–39

Pray that we would walk in victory, not as victims of circumstance, but as overcomers empowered by the Holy Spirit, anchored in God's love.

Ask that we will grasp the full meaning of being more than conquerors through Christ who loves us.

_____

_____

_____

_____

_____

_____

_____

_____

_____

_____

_____

_____

_____

_____

_____

_____

_____

_____

The Great Commission

Pray for those who have answered the call to full-time ministry and are facing trials, opposition, or personal loss.

Ask that they be strengthened by the deep knowledge of God's unfailing love and sustained by His abiding presence in every circumstance.

Pray they do not grow weary but that they will be refreshed and encouraged in their calling.

_____

_____

_____

_____

_____

_____

_____

_____

_____

_____

_____

_____

_____

_____

_____

_____

_____

_____

Prayer for Others

Pray for someone in your circle of friends or family who is facing loss, grief, or uncertainty.

Ask God to surround them with His peace that surpasses all understanding, to comfort their heart, strengthen their faith, and guide them through this difficult season.

Pray that His presence would be their anchor, and that they would find renewed hope and assurance in His promises.

_____

_____

_____

_____

_____

_____

_____

_____

_____

_____

_____

_____

_____

_____

_____

_____

Thank God for the unshakable security found in His love.

Thank Him for the steady guidance of His hand, and the living hope you carry as His beloved child.

Rejoice in the assurance that He is always with you, leading you with purpose and covering you with grace.

_____

_____

_____

_____

_____

_____

_____

_____

_____

_____

_____

_____

_____

_____

_____

_____

_____

_____

**Weekly
Scripture
Focus**

"Being confident of this very thing, that He who has begun a good work in you will complete it until the day of Jesus Christ." Philippians 1:6

"And they overcame him by the blood of the Lamb and by the word of their testimony, and they did not love their lives to the death." Revelation 12:11

As your prayer begins this week, lift up praise to God for His recent provision, and repent of wrongdoing—praying on behalf of yourself, others, the Church, and your nation.

_____

_____

_____

_____

_____

_____

_____

_____

_____

_____

_____

_____

_____

_____

_____

_____

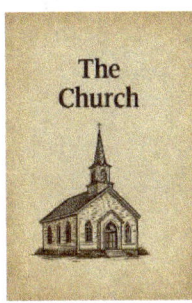

The Church

Pray that the Body of Christ would be fully equipped for every good work, walking in obedience and bearing fruit that glorifies God.

Ask the Lord to bring spiritual growth and maturity to His people, and to strengthen them with power and endurance, so they may serve faithfully with perseverance and joy.

_____

_____

_____

_____

_____

_____

_____

_____

_____

_____

_____

_____

_____

_____

_____

_____

_____

_____

_____

_____

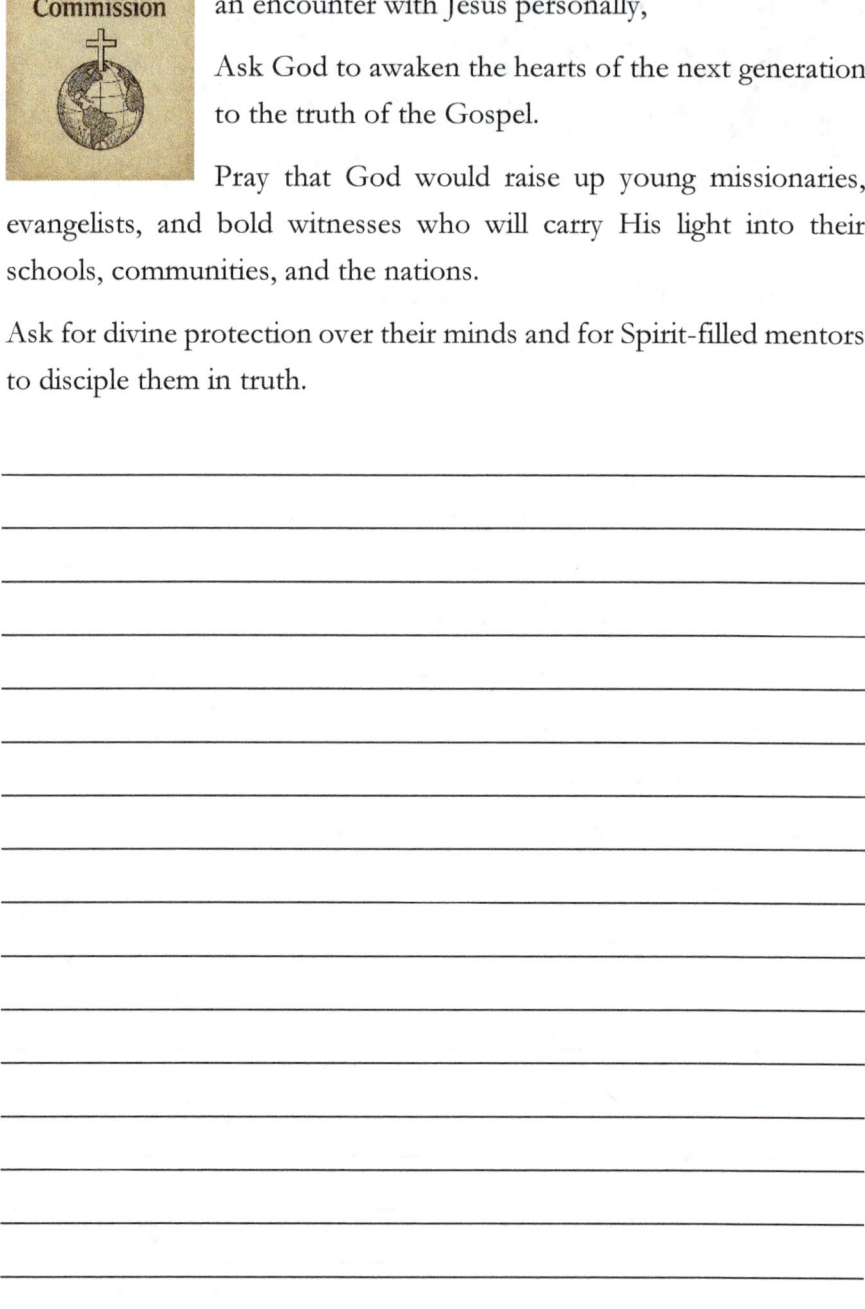

The Great Commission

Pray for children and youth to be reached with the good news of the Gospel, and that they would have an encounter with Jesus personally,

Ask God to awaken the hearts of the next generation to the truth of the Gospel.

Pray that God would raise up young missionaries, evangelists, and bold witnesses who will carry His light into their schools, communities, and the nations.

Ask for divine protection over their minds and for Spirit-filled mentors to disciple them in truth.

_____

_____

_____

_____

_____

_____

_____

_____

_____

_____

_____

_____

_____

_____

_____

_____

_____

Prayer for Others

Think of someone you know who is experiencing tension or hardship within their family.

Ask the Lord to bring healing, restoration, and peace to their home.

Pray that His love would mend broken relationships, soften hearts, and bring unity where there is division.

As you come into God's presence today, humbly remind Him of the answers to prayers you are still waiting on.

Thank Him for His faithfulness, and trust that in His perfect timing, He will bring every promise to fulfillment.

Weekly Scripture Focus

"That you may walk worthy of the Lord, fully pleasing Him, being fruitful in every good work and increasing in the knowledge of God; strengthened with all might, according to His glorious power, for all patience and longsuffering with joy."
Colossians 1:10-11

As your prayer begins this week, lift up praise to God for His recent provision, and repent of wrongdoing—praying on behalf of yourself, others, the Church, and your nation.

_____

_____

_____

_____

_____

_____

_____

_____

_____

_____

_____

_____

_____

_____

_____

_____

The Church

Pray that we live lives worthy of the high price Jesus paid for our redemption—walking in holiness, gratitude, and purpose.

Pray that Christ's character will be fully formed in us, reflecting His love, humility, and obedience.

Pray that we would endure faithfully to the end and finish strong, fulfilling the calling and purpose God has placed on our lives.

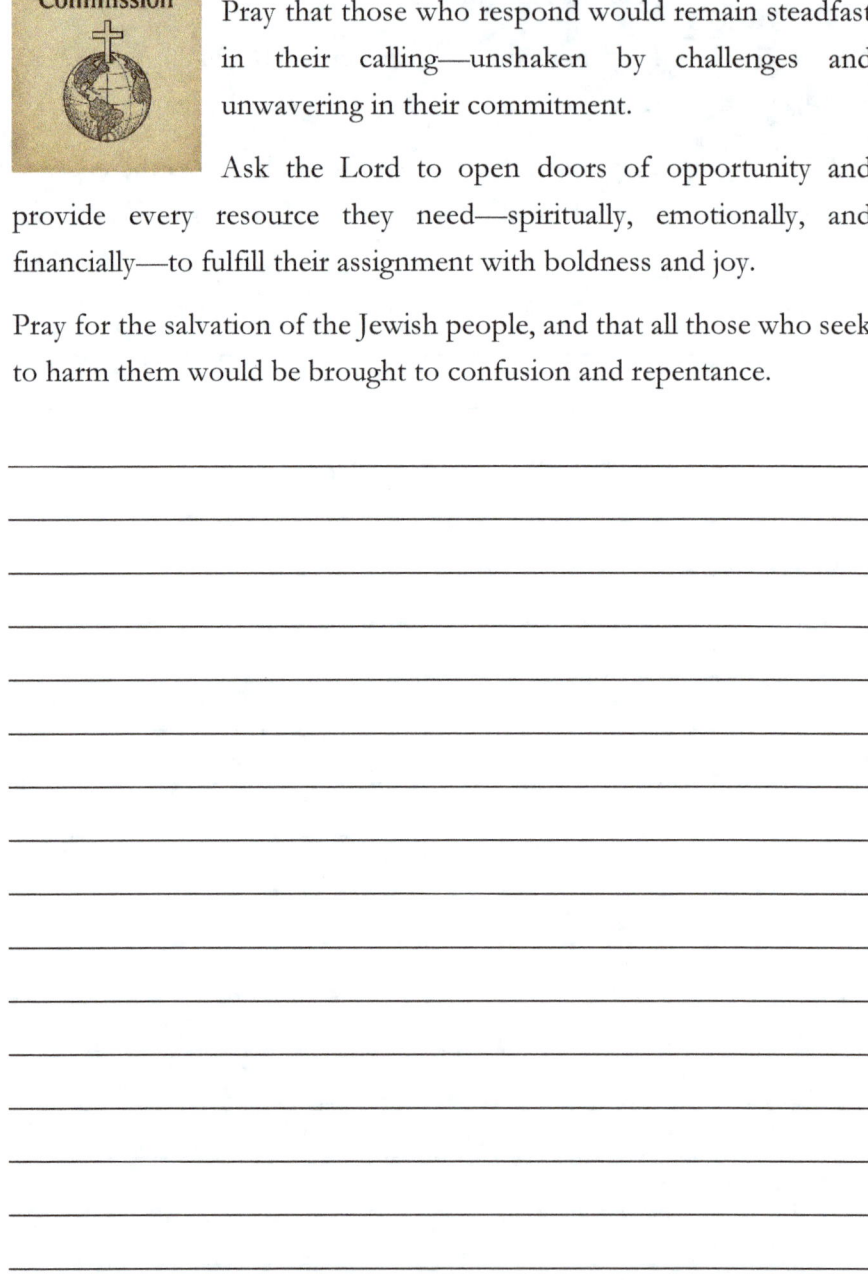

The Great Commission

Ask the Holy Spirit to call and awaken hearts to serve as workers in God's harvest field.

Pray that those who respond would remain steadfast in their calling—unshaken by challenges and unwavering in their commitment.

Ask the Lord to open doors of opportunity and provide every resource they need—spiritually, emotionally, and financially—to fulfill their assignment with boldness and joy.

Pray for the salvation of the Jewish people, and that all those who seek to harm them would be brought to confusion and repentance.

Prayer for Others

Think of someone you know who has grown cold in their faith or is drifting away from God.

Ask the Holy Spirit to lovingly convict their heart, awaken their spiritual hunger, and draw them back into close fellowship with Him.

Pray that every distraction or disappointment would be removed, and that they would be reminded of God's unfailing love and purpose for their life.

If possible, reach out to them—offer encouragement, remind them they are not alone, and let them know you are standing with them in prayer.

_____

_____

_____

_____

_____

_____

_____

_____

_____

_____

_____

_____

_____

_____

"Create in me a clean heart, O God, and renew a steadfast spirit within me.

Do not cast me from your presence, and do not take your Holy Spirit from me.

Restore to me the joy of Your salvation, and uphold me by Your generous spirit."

Psalm 51:10-12

May my life reflect your glory.

_____

_____

_____

_____

_____

_____

_____

_____

_____

_____

_____

_____

_____

_____

_____

_____

_____

_____

Weekly Scripture Focus

"The Lord is my shepherd; I shall not want.

He makes me to lie down in green pastures; He leads me beside the still waters.

He restores my soul; He leads me in the paths of righteousness for His name's sake.

Yea, though I walk through the valley of the shadow of death, I will fear no evil; for You are with me; Your rod and Your staff, they comfort me.

You prepare a table before me in the presence of my enemies; You anoint my head with oil; my cup runs over.

Surely goodness and mercy shall follow me all the days of my life; and I will dwell in the house of the Lord forever." Psalm 23:1-6

As your prayer begins this week, lift up praise to God for His recent provision, and repent of wrongdoing—praying on behalf of yourself, others, the Church, and your nation.

_____

_____

_____

_____

_____

_____

_____

_____

_____

_____

The Church

Trust the Lord, our Shepherd, fully—trust His care, provision, and guidance.

Enter His rest, be free from anxiety and striving, follow His voice daily.

Thank the Lord for His faithful leading, through valleys and unknown paths, and that His goodness and mercy continually follow us, sustaining us all the days of our lives.

_____

_____

_____

_____

_____

_____

_____

_____

_____

_____

_____

_____

_____

_____

_____

_____

_____

_____

_____

The Great Commission

Psalm 23 is a universally comforting Scripture, reminding us that the Lord is our Shepherd. Yet there are still people in remote regions—like among the Inuit communities of the Arctic—who may not have heard the Good Shepherd's voice.

Pray for missionaries called to these isolated and often harsh environments.

Ask God to equip them with wisdom, endurance, and cultural sensitivity.

Pray that hearts will be open, and that the truth of God's Word will reach even the furthest corners of the earth.

_____

_____

_____

_____

_____

_____

_____

_____

_____

_____

_____

_____

_____

_____

Prayer for Others

Ask God to lead you to someone who is lost or searching—someone who needs to know Jesus as the Good Shepherd.

Pray for a divine opportunity to share the Good News with them, and that your words would carry His love, truth, and hope.

_____

_____

_____

_____

_____

_____

_____

_____

_____

_____

_____

_____

_____

_____

_____

_____

_____

_____

_____

_____

_____

Thank God for the table He has prepared before you, even in the presence of your enemies.

Praise Him for His unfailing goodness and steadfast mercy that follows you all the days of your life.

Acknowledge His abundant provision, protection, and the peace that surrounds you because you belong to Him.

_____

_____

_____

_____

_____

_____

_____

_____

_____

_____

_____

_____

_____

_____

_____

_____

_____

_____

The Faith Race

"Therefore we also, since we are surrounded by so great a cloud of witnesses, let us lay aside every weight, and the sin which so easily ensnares us, and let us run with endurance the race that is set before us, looking unto Jesus, the author and finisher of our faith, who for the joy that was set before Him endured the cross, despising the shame, and has sat down at the right hand of the throne of God." Hebrews 12:1-2

As your prayer begins this week, lift up praise to God for His recent provision, and repent of wrongdoing—praying on behalf of yourself, others, the Church, and your nation.

_____

_____

_____

_____

_____

_____

_____

_____

_____

_____

_____

_____

_____

_____

The Church

Pray that as believers, we would bear the fruit of faith which is faithfulness.

Ask the Holy Spirit for help as we run the race with endurance, keeping our eyes fixed on the goal—Jesus Christ.

Pray that we would continually look to Jesus, the Author and Finisher of our faith, drawing strength and direction from Him.

The Great Commission

Pray that wherever the Gospel is preached, the message would fall on good and receptive soil—on hearts that are ready to receive the truth.

Ask God to prepare hearts ahead of time, so that lasting decisions will be made to follow Christ.

Pray that as His people, we would sow the seed generously, boldly, and without hesitation, trusting God for a bountiful harvest.

Prayer for Others

Pray for those relationships closest to you.

If you are married, pray for your spouse.

Ask God to bless, strengthen, and protect your marriage.

Single? Pray for your family—ask God to draw their hearts closer to Him.

Grandparent? Intercede for your grandchildren—pray that they would walk in truth, be protected from harm, and come to know and love Jesus deeply from a young age.

_____

_____

_____

_____

_____

_____

_____

_____

_____

_____

_____

_____

_____

_____

_____

_____

_____

If you are trusting God for something, bring your request before Him again today with faith.

Remind Him of His promises and believe that *"Now to Him who is able to do exceedingly abundantly above all that we ask or think, according to the power that works in us."* Ephesians 3:20.

Weekly Scripture Focus

"Be still, and know that I am God; I will be exalted among the nations, I will be exalted in the earth!

The Lord of hosts is with us; The God of Jacob is our refuge. Selah." Psalm 46:10-11

As your prayer begins this week, lift up praise to God for His recent provision, and repent of wrongdoing—praying on behalf of yourself, others, the Church, and your nation.

_____

_____

_____

_____

_____

_____

_____

_____

_____

_____

_____

_____

_____

_____

_____

_____

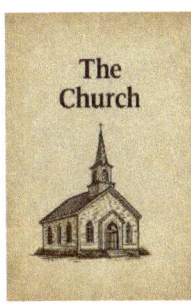

The Church

Declare that the Lord of Hosts is with us, He is our mighty defender, our commander in battle, and our ever-present help in times of need.

Thank Him for being our refuge and strength, a strong tower we can run to in times of trouble, where we are safe and secure.

Pray that we would walk in unshakable confidence, knowing that the God of angel armies surrounds and upholds us.

_____

_____

_____

_____

_____

_____

_____

_____

_____

_____

_____

_____

_____

_____

_____

_____

_____

The Great Commission ✝

The Great Commission often begins at the very place of your deepest failure—just as it did for the disciples, who were called to be witnesses in Jerusalem, the city where they had denied, abandoned, and doubted Jesus. Yet it was there that grace met them, restored them, and empowered them to proclaim the Gospel.

Pray that God would use your place of brokenness as a platform for His power. Ask the Holy Spirit to give you boldness to be a faithful witness—right where you are.

Prayer for Others

Pray for busy moms:

Ask God to strengthen them and give them peace and patience as they nurture their families.

Pray that they would feel supported, refreshed, and empowered by His presence in every task, big or small.

_____

_____

_____

_____

_____

_____

_____

_____

_____

_____

_____

_____

_____

_____

_____

_____

_____

_____

_____

_____

_____

Ask God to quiet your heart and still your spirit to hear His voice clearly above all distractions.

Pray for a posture of peace and attentiveness, ready to receive His guidance.

Weekly Scripture Focus

"For this reason I bow my knees to the Father of our Lord Jesus Christ, from whom the whole family in heaven and earth is named, that He would grant you, according to the riches of His glory, to be strengthened with might through His Spirit in the inner man, that Christ may dwell in your hearts through faith; that you, being rooted and grounded in love, may be able to comprehend with all the saints what is the width and length and depth and height— to know the love of Christ which passes knowledge; that you may be filled with all the fullness of God. Now to Him who is able to do exceedingly abundantly above all that we ask or think, according to the power that works in us, to Him be glory in the church by Christ Jesus to all generations, forever and ever. Amen." Ephesians 3:14-21

As your prayer begins this week, lift up praise to God for His recent provision, and repent of wrongdoing—praying on behalf of yourself, others, the Church, and your nation.

_____

_____

_____

_____

_____

_____

_____

_____

_____

_____

_____

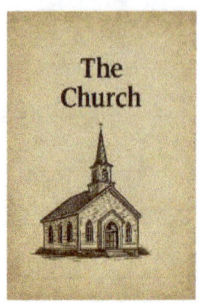

The Church

Pray for those whom God has called out of darkness into His marvelous light.

Pray that the Word of God will take deep root in their hearts and transform them.

Pray that as they hear God's Word preached, they would flourish in faith, grow in grace, and bear lasting fruit for the Kingdom.

The Great Commission

Pray for prison ministries around the world—that they would be filled with compassion and wisdom as they bring hope to the hopeless.

Ask God to open doors for practical ministry opportunities to meet the spiritual and physical needs of those who are incarcerated.

Prayer for Others

Ask the Lord to show you how to serve someone with kindness, generosity, or a simple act of love today.

Pray that through it, their heart would be drawn to Jesus.

May your actions reflect His compassion and open a door for a deeper relationship with Him.

_____

_____

_____

_____

_____

_____

_____

_____

_____

_____

_____

_____

_____

_____

_____

_____

_____

_____

_____

Choose a Psalm and pray it out loud as an act of worship.

Declare its truths as a personal song of praise to God, letting His Word shape your adoration and strengthen your faith.

_____

_____

_____

_____

_____

_____

_____

_____

_____

_____

_____

_____

_____

_____

_____

_____

_____

_____

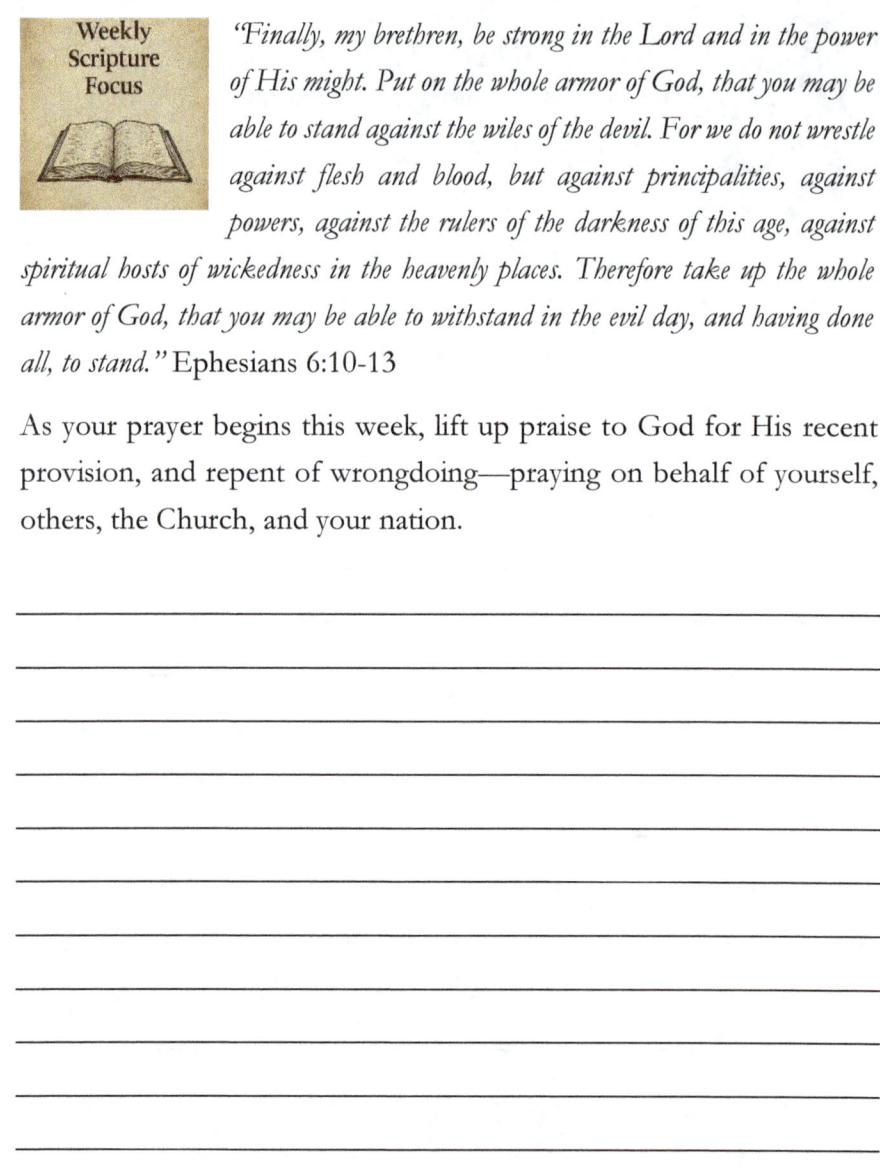

Weekly Scripture Focus

"Finally, my brethren, be strong in the Lord and in the power of His might. Put on the whole armor of God, that you may be able to stand against the wiles of the devil. For we do not wrestle against flesh and blood, but against principalities, against powers, against the rulers of the darkness of this age, against spiritual hosts of wickedness in the heavenly places. Therefore take up the whole armor of God, that you may be able to withstand in the evil day, and having done all, to stand." Ephesians 6:10-13

As your prayer begins this week, lift up praise to God for His recent provision, and repent of wrongdoing—praying on behalf of yourself, others, the Church, and your nation.

_____

_____

_____

_____

_____

_____

_____

_____

_____

_____

_____

_____

_____

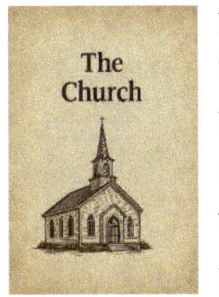

The Church

Pray that believers would put on the Lord Jesus Christ as protection.

Pray that we will understand the battle is not against flesh and blood but rather against spiritual hosts of wickedness.

Pray that we stand firm in truth, righteousness, salvation, and all the spiritual weapons we have as God's children.

_____

_____

_____

_____

_____

_____

_____

_____

_____

_____

_____

_____

_____

_____

_____

_____

_____

_____

_____

_____

_____

_____

The Great Commission

Pray that missionaries sent to difficult and unreached regions would bear much fruit, establishing strong, Spirit-filled churches that will stand as beacons of truth.

Pray that the truth of the Word, the shield of faith, and the sword of the Spirit is used effectively as they share the Gospel of peace.

Ask God to open doors that no man can shut, and confirm His Word with signs, wonders, and a powerful manifestation of His presence.

Prayer for Others

Ask God to fill your heart with His compassion for those who are held captive—whether by sin, addiction, fear, or spiritual blindness—and to give you His perspective of mercy and love.

Pray that every chain of bondage would be broken by the power of Jesus' name, and that those walking in darkness would be set free and brought into His marvelous light.

_____

_____

_____

_____

_____

_____

_____

_____

_____

_____

_____

_____

_____

_____

_____

_____

_____

_____

Ask God to give you discernment to recognize distractions or unnecessary battles the enemy may try to draw you into.

Put on the whole armor of God and ask Him for help to stand firm in faith, rooted in His Word and unwavering in your purpose.

Weekly Scripture Focus

"Stand therefore, having girded your waist with truth, having put on the breastplate of righteousness, and having shod your feet with the preparation of the gospel of peace; above all, taking the shield of faith with which you will be able to quench all the fiery darts of the wicked one. And take the helmet of salvation, and the sword of the Spirit, which is the word of God; praying always with all prayer and supplication in the Spirit, being watchful to this end with all perseverance and supplication for all the saints— and for me, that utterance may be given to me, that I may open my mouth boldly to make known the mystery of the gospel, for which I am an ambassador in chains; that in it I may speak boldly, as I ought to speak." Ephesians 6:14-20

As your prayer begins this week, lift up praise to God for His recent provision, and repent of wrongdoing—praying on behalf of yourself, others, the Church, and your nation.

_____

_____

_____

_____

_____

_____

_____

_____

_____

_____

_____

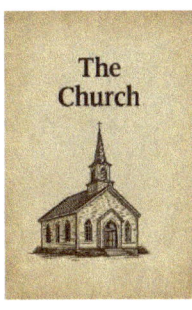

The Church

Pray that as believers, we would stand our ground putting on the belt of truth, and the body armor of God's righteousness.

Pray that every lie of the enemy to bind or deceive us will be exposed.

Declare: *"The truth shall make you free."* John 8:32

Declare: *"Yet in all these things we are more than conquerors through Him who loved us."* Romans 8:37

The Great Commission

Pray for those imprisoned for the sake of the Gospel—that they would be filled with supernatural boldness, even greater behind prison walls than in freedom.

Pray that their witness would shine brightly, bringing hope, salvation, and revival to fellow inmates and prison staff alike.

_____
_____
_____
_____
_____
_____
_____
_____
_____
_____
_____
_____
_____
_____
_____
_____
_____
_____

Prayer for Others

Pray for Christian men everywhere—that they would rise up as godly leaders, in the community and in their homes, that they would love their wives with Christlike devotion, and faithfully train their children to know, love, and serve the Lord.

Ask God to open your eyes to what it truly means to be spiritually watchful, alert in prayer, steadfast in faith, and persistent in intercession.

Pray for the strength to persevere and the compassion to faithfully make supplication for all God's people.

_____

_____

_____

_____

_____

_____

_____

_____

_____

_____

_____

_____

_____

_____

_____

_____

_____

_____

_____

_____

Weekly Scripture Focus

"How shall we escape if we neglect so great a salvation, which at the first began to be spoken by the Lord, and was confirmed to us by those who heard Him," Hebrews 2:3

As your prayer begins this week, lift up praise to God for His recent provision, and repent of wrongdoing—praying on behalf of yourself, others, the Church, and your nation.

_____

_____

_____

_____

_____

_____

_____

_____

_____

_____

_____

_____

_____

_____

_____

_____

_____

_____

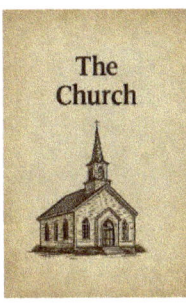

The Church

Pray for those who are double-minded. Ask the Holy Spirit to establish them in wholehearted devotion to God.

Intercede for those battling unbelief. Ask the Holy Spirit to strengthen their faith and anchor them in God's promises.

Pray for those whose hearts have grown cold. Ask the Holy Spirit to draw them back.

"Not lagging in diligence, fervent in spirit, serving the Lord." Romans 12:11

The Great Commission

Pray for missionaries and church planters working in challenging regions.

Ask God to give them divine strategies tailored to the cultures they serve, supernatural grace to learn and speak the local languages, deep favor with the communities they reach, and lasting, Spirit-led fruit that multiplies disciples and churches.

_____

_____

_____

_____

_____

_____

_____

_____

_____

_____

_____

_____

_____

_____

_____

_____

_____

_____

_____

Prayer for Others

Pray for those who are struggling with illness.

Ask God to bring healing, comfort, and strength to their body, mind, and spirit. Pray that His presence would surround them, His peace would sustain them, and His power would restore them fully.

_____

_____

_____

_____

_____

_____

_____

_____

_____

_____

_____

_____

_____

_____

_____

_____

_____

_____

_____

_____

Ask God to keep your heart tender and responsive to Him—guarding you from spiritual apathy, renewing your first love, and setting your soul ablaze with fresh passion for His presence.

_____

_____

_____

_____

_____

_____

_____

_____

_____

_____

_____

_____

_____

_____

_____

_____

_____

_____

Weekly Scripture Focus

"Therefore, my beloved brethren, be steadfast, immovable, always abounding in the work of the Lord, knowing that your labor is not in vain in the Lord." 1 Corinthians 15:58

As your prayer begins this week, lift up praise to God for His recent provision, and repent of wrongdoing—praying on behalf of yourself, others, the Church, and your nation.

_____

_____

_____

_____

_____

_____

_____

_____

_____

_____

_____

_____

_____

_____

_____

_____

_____

_____

_____

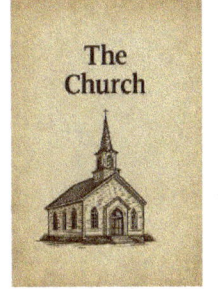

The Church

Pray for pastors, that they would be courageous.

Pray for godly character and that they will remain faithful to their calling.

Ask the Holy Spirit to empower them daily as they shepherd God's people.

When it comes to those who are in full time work, Satan tempts and entices them in many ways.

There are times that they feel dejected and tired, as the labor is hard and sometimes seems fruitless. It is a known fact that fifty percent of those who go into full-time ministry quit after the first year. We must remember to pray for them continually. Paul asked believers to join him in this struggle by asking for prayer for himself.

_____

_____

_____

_____

_____

_____

_____

_____

_____

_____

_____

_____

_____

_____

The Great Commission

Pray for missions—both locally and globally.

Lift up those reaching communities with the Gospel.

Especially pray for the mission efforts you are personally connected to.

Ask God to empower them with wisdom, provision, and lasting impact, and many salvations.

Prayer for Others

Are you thinking of someone today?

Don't dismiss it as a coincidence—see it as the Holy Spirit prompting you to pray.

Lift that person before the throne of grace.

Ask God to surround them with His protection, provide for their every need, and draw them closer to Himself.

_____

_____

_____

_____

_____

_____

_____

_____

_____

_____

_____

_____

_____

_____

_____

_____

_____

_____

_____

Thank God for His Word, which is a lamp to your feet and a light to your path. Praise Him for the truth that sets you free and the power of His Spirit that enables you to be a bold witness.

Give thanks for daily guidance, wisdom, and faithful direction in every step you take.

Ask Him for increase in all these areas.

_____

_____

_____

_____

_____

_____

_____

_____

_____

_____

_____

_____

_____

_____

_____

_____

_____

_____

_____

Weekly
Scripture
Focus

"Praying always with all prayer and supplication in the Spirit, being watchful to this end with all perseverance and supplication for all the saints." Ephesians 6:18

As your prayer begins this week, lift up praise to God for His recent provision, and repent of wrongdoing—praying on behalf of yourself, others, the Church, and your nation.

_____

_____

_____

_____

_____

_____

_____

_____

_____

_____

_____

_____

_____

_____

_____

_____

_____

_____

_____

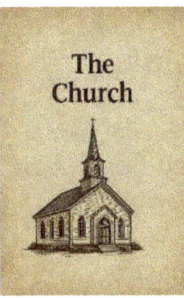

The Church

For those struggling with health:

Pray for healing, strength, and renewed hope, as they are battling physical, emotional, or mental illness.

Ask that they would experience God's peace, comfort, and sustaining grace in every season of weakness.

_____

_____

_____

_____

_____

_____

_____

_____

_____

_____

_____

_____

_____

_____

_____

_____

_____

_____

_____

_____

The Great Commission

Pray for your church service this week—that as the Gospel is boldly proclaimed, every stronghold would be broken, and those bound by fear, sin, or oppression would experience true freedom in Christ.

Pray for the salvation of the Jewish people, and that all those who seek to harm them would be brought to confusion and repentance.

_____
_____
_____
_____
_____
_____
_____
_____
_____
_____
_____
_____
_____
_____
_____
_____
_____
_____
_____

Prayer for Others

Pray for the neighbors living near you.

Ask God to open doors for you to share the Gospel with them.

Pray for opportunities to show Christ's love through practical acts of kindness that demonstrate genuine care and build trust.

_____

_____

_____

_____

_____

_____

_____

_____

_____

_____

_____

_____

_____

_____

_____

_____

_____

_____

_____

_____

Ask the Holy Spirit to fix your mind on the things of the Spirit and to help you release every burden that is not yours to carry.

Pray for clarity, peace, and renewed focus on what truly matters.

_____

_____

_____

_____

_____

_____

_____

_____

_____

_____

_____

_____

_____

_____

_____

_____

_____

_____

Weekly Scripture Focus

"Intercessions should first of all be made for those who are in authority, so that we may live in peace and preach the Gospel.

Therefore I exhort first of all those supplications, prayers, intercessions, and giving of thanks be made for all men, for kings and all who are in authority, that we may lead a quiet and peaceable life in all godliness and reverence. For this is good and acceptable in the sight of God our Savior, who desires all men to be saved and to come to the knowledge of the truth."
1 Timothy 2:1-4

As your prayer begins this week, lift up praise to God for His recent provision, and repent of wrongdoing—praying on behalf of yourself, others, the Church, and your nation.

_____

_____

_____

_____

_____

_____

_____

_____

_____

_____

_____

_____

_____

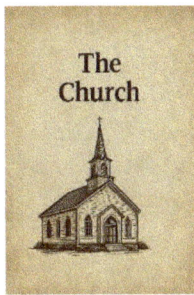

The Church

Pray for single adults desiring a life partner.

Pray that they would trust God's perfect timing and wait patiently with hope.

Ask the Lord to prepare their hearts and the hearts of those they are meant to join with, and that their desire for companionship would be fulfilled according to His will, bringing glory to His name.

_____
_____
_____
_____
_____
_____
_____
_____
_____
_____
_____
_____
_____
_____
_____
_____
_____
_____
_____
_____

The Great Commission

But Jesus said, "Let the little children come to Me, and do not forbid them; for of such is the kingdom of heaven." Matthew 19:14. He longs to bless them.

Pray for those who are faithfully sharing the Gospel with children.

Ask God to captivate young hearts at an early age and draw them into a lifelong relationship with Him

_____

_____

_____

_____

_____

_____

_____

_____

_____

_____

_____

_____

_____

_____

_____

_____

_____

_____

_____

_____

Prayer for Others

Pray for those in positions of authority—national leaders, public servants, and judges.

Ask God to guide their thoughts and decisions with wisdom and righteousness.

Pray for their salvation, that they would come to know Christ and lead with integrity and justice.1 Timothy 2:1-2

_____

_____

_____

_____

_____

_____

_____

_____

_____

_____

_____

_____

_____

_____

_____

_____

_____

_____

_____

Give thanks for the many ways God has brought peace into your life—through His presence, His promises, and His provision.

Take time to write down the blessings you're thankful for, and let gratitude fill your heart and prayers.

_____

_____

_____

_____

_____

_____

_____

_____

_____

_____

_____

_____

_____

_____

_____

_____

_____

_____

_____

_____

Weekly Scripture Focus

"But you shall receive power when the Holy Spirit has come upon you; and you shall be witnesses to Me in Jerusalem, and in all Judea and Samaria, and to the end of the earth." Acts 1:8

As your prayer begins this week, lift up praise to God for His recent provision, and repent of wrongdoing—praying on behalf of yourself, others, the Church, and your nation.

_____

_____

_____

_____

_____

_____

_____

_____

_____

_____

_____

_____

_____

_____

_____

_____

_____

The Church

Pray for every person in our church to receive the baptism of the Holy Spirit and become a powerful witness.

_____

_____

_____

_____

_____

_____

_____

_____

_____

_____

_____

_____

_____

_____

_____

_____

_____

_____

_____

_____

_____

_____

The Great Commission

Lift up the teachers, administrators, and all who shape the minds and hearts of children.

Pray for educators who are wise, faithful, and committed to truth and righteousness.

Pray that any ungodly influence or agenda that seeks to confuse, corrupt, or disrupt the moral foundation of the next generation would be removed.

Ask the Lord to protect our children and to plant them in environments where they can grow in wisdom, character, and faith.

_____
_____
_____
_____
_____
_____
_____
_____
_____
_____
_____
_____
_____
_____
_____
_____
_____
_____

Prayer for Others

Family is God's divine design and a precious gift. As you reflect on the family God has placed you in, take time to pray for each member.

Lift up your parents, siblings, and extended family, asking the Lord to bless, protect, and draw them closer to Him. Remember—God deeply loves your family and desires to work powerfully in and through them.

_____

_____

_____

_____

_____

_____

_____

_____

_____

_____

_____

_____

_____

_____

_____

_____

_____

_____

_____

Ask God to bless and multiply what you bring to Him—your time, resources, and talents—so that you may have more than enough: enough to meet your needs, to share with others, and to sow generously into His Kingdom.

Pray for a heart that reflects His generous nature, overflowing with kindness, compassion, and open-handed giving.

_____

_____

_____

_____

_____

_____

_____

_____

_____

_____

_____

_____

_____

_____

_____

_____

_____

_____

Weekly Scripture Focus

"But without faith it is impossible to please Him, for he who comes to God must believe that He is, and that He is a rewarder of those who diligently seek Him." Hebrews 11:6

"Let us therefore come boldly to the throne of grace, that we may obtain mercy and find grace to help in time of need." Hebrews 4:16

As your prayer begins this week, lift up praise to God for His recent provision, and repent of wrongdoing—praying on behalf of yourself, others, the Church, and your nation.

_____

_____

_____

_____

_____

_____

_____

_____

_____

_____

_____

_____

_____

_____

_____

_____

The Church

Pray that as believers, we should seek first the Kingdom of God and His righteousness.

Ask the Lord to align our priorities with His—putting His will, His purposes, and His rule above all else.

Pray that we would trust Him to provide all that we need as we live with a Kingdom-first mindset. Matthew 6:33

The Great Commission

When the Gospel is preached, God confirms His Word with signs, wonders, and miracles—demonstrating His love and power to those who do not yet know Him.

Pray for faith to believe Him for these manifestations today and ask that His gifts would flow through our lives as a testimony to His goodness and truth.

_____

_____

_____

_____

_____

_____

_____

_____

_____

_____

_____

_____

_____

_____

_____

_____

_____

_____

_____

Prayer for Others

God deeply loves people—even those who are difficult to love. Sometimes He places these individuals in our lives so we can reflect His love and compassion. Often, their hardness is a shield from past wounds.

Pray that the Holy Spirit will use you as an instrument of healing and grace, breaking through their walls with kindness, and leading them toward wholeness in Christ.

Scripture encourages us to come boldly to God's throne of grace with our requests. He is a loving Father who delights in hearing from His children, so bring your requests to Him in faith. As the Word says, *"Yet you do not have because you do not ask."* James 4:2

Ask—trusting that He hears you and desires to respond according to His perfect will.

_____

_____

_____

_____

_____

_____

_____

_____

_____

_____

_____

_____

_____

_____

_____

_____

_____

_____

Weekly Scripture Focus

"Again, I say to you that if two of you agree on earth concerning anything that they ask, it will be done for them by My Father in heaven. For where two or three are gathered together in My name, I am there in the midst of them." Matthew 18:19-20

As your prayer begins this week, lift up praise to God for His recent provision, and repent of wrongdoing—praying on behalf of yourself, others, the Church, and your nation.

_____

_____

_____

_____

_____

_____

_____

_____

_____

_____

_____

_____

_____

_____

_____

_____

_____

_____

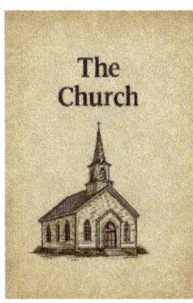

The Church

Pray that as believers, we would be in full agreement with the will of the Lord.

Ask God to align us in purpose, vision, and spirit.

Thank the Lord that our unity is found in Christ Jesus—He is our common ground, our peace, and the One who holds us together.

Pray that our unity would glorify Him and bear lasting fruit.

_____

_____

_____

_____

_____

_____

_____

_____

_____

_____

_____

_____

_____

_____

_____

_____

_____

_____

_____

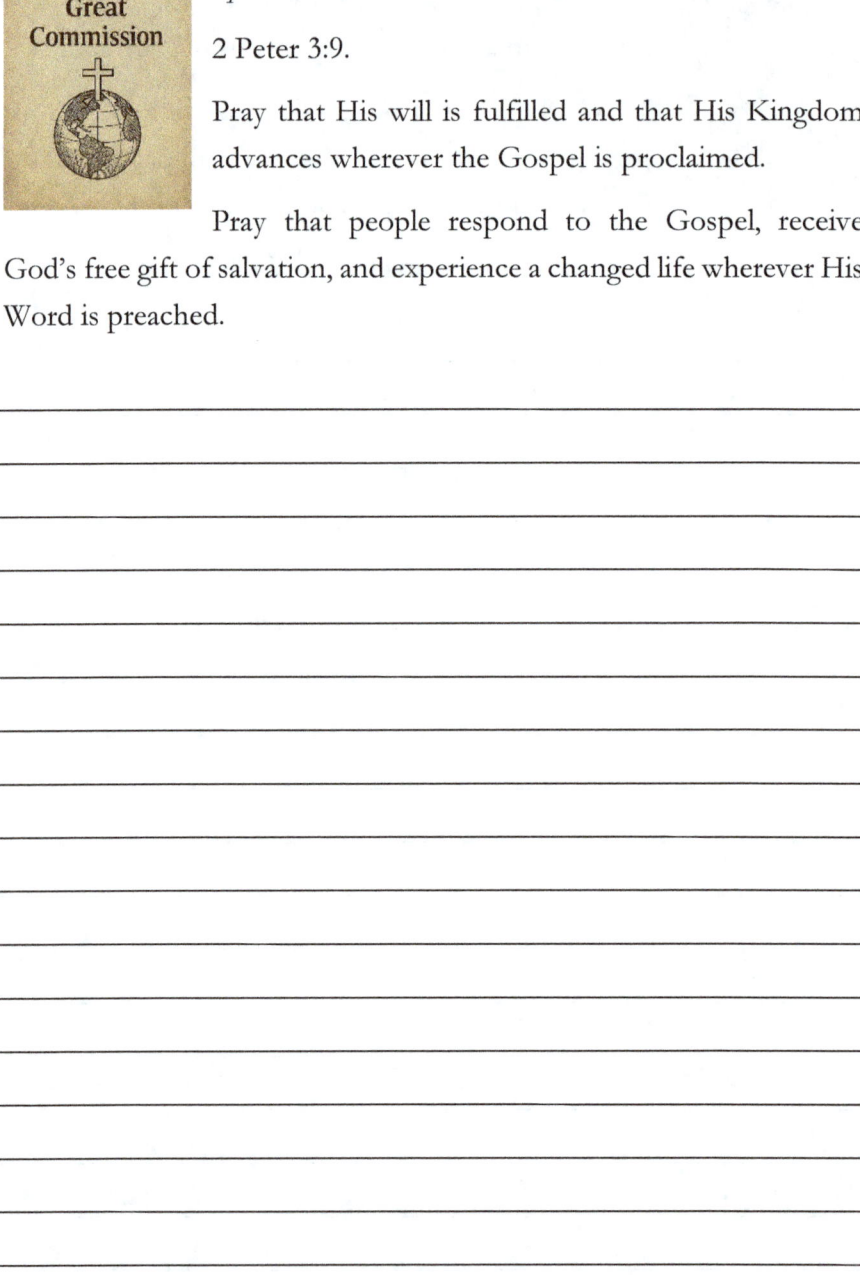

The Great Commission

"Not willing that any should perish but that all should come to repentance."

2 Peter 3:9.

Pray that His will is fulfilled and that His Kingdom advances wherever the Gospel is proclaimed.

Pray that people respond to the Gospel, receive God's free gift of salvation, and experience a changed life wherever His Word is preached.

_____

_____

_____

_____

_____

_____

_____

_____

_____

_____

_____

_____

_____

_____

_____

_____

_____

Prayer for Others

If you work in an office or spend time with co-workers each day, remember that someone around you likely carries a hidden burden. Be sensitive to the prompting of the Holy Spirit—people may appear fine on the outside but be struggling on the inside.

Quietly pray for them, trusting that God sees, knows, and can meet their needs through your intercession. Even if they never know you prayed, God calls you to be faithful.

Pray, "Lord, turn my heart like rivers of water—soften and guide it according to Your will.

"Shape my desires, direct my thoughts, and lead me in the paths that please You."

_____
_____
_____
_____
_____
_____
_____
_____
_____
_____
_____
_____
_____
_____
_____
_____
_____
_____

Weekly Scripture Focus

The Parable of the Persistent Widow:

"Then He spoke a parable to them, that men always ought to pray and not lose heart, saying: 'There was in a certain city a judge who did not fear God nor regard man.' Now there was a widow in that city; and she came to him, saying, 'Get justice for me from my adversary.' And he would not for a while; but afterward he said within himself, 'Though I do not fear God nor regard man, yet because this widow troubles me I will avenge her, lest by her continual coming she weary me.' Then the Lord said, 'Hear what the unjust judge said. And shall God not avenge His own elect who cry out day and night to Him, though He bears long with them? I tell you that He will avenge them speedily. Nevertheless, when the Son of Man comes, will He really find faith on the earth?'" Luke 18:1-8.

As your prayer begins this week, lift up praise to God for His recent provision, and repent of wrongdoing—praying on behalf of yourself, others, the Church, and your nation.

_____

_____

_____

_____

_____

_____

_____

_____

The Church

Pray that we would be steadfast and persistent in our walk with God—never giving up, even during life's trials.

Pray that we would be rooted and established in the faith, holding firmly to the hope we profess.

Pray that we would endure to the end of our race, becoming mature and complete in Christ. James 1:4.

_____

_____

_____

_____

_____

_____

_____

_____

_____

_____

_____

_____

_____

_____

_____

_____

_____

_____

_____

The Great Commission

Pray for the multitudes in the valley of decision. Joel 3:14

Ask the Holy Spirit to bring deep conviction to those who are undecided about Christ.

Pray that the lies of the enemy would be exposed, and God's truth would shine clearly.

Ask the Lord to anoint preachers, evangelists, and ordinary believers to speak the truth in love.

_____

_____

_____

_____

_____

_____

_____

_____

_____

_____

_____

_____

_____

_____

_____

_____

_____

_____

Prayer for Others

If you work for a company, pray for your boss.

Ask God to bless them with wisdom and integrity. If they do not yet know the Lord, pray for their salvation.

Pray that your life would be a light, reflecting Christ's love and truth in the workplace.

_____

_____

_____

_____

_____

_____

_____

_____

_____

_____

_____

_____

_____

_____

_____

_____

_____

_____

_____

Jesus said, "Watch and pray." Ask the Holy Spirit to show you how to be spiritually alert and discerning so that your prayers are timely and effective.

Pray for a heart that is sensitive to the needs of others as you watch.

Ask the Holy Spirit to increase your burden to intercede with compassion and urgency.

_____

_____

_____

_____

_____

_____

_____

_____

_____

_____

_____

_____

_____

_____

_____

_____

_____

Weekly Scripture Focus

"But we all, with unveiled face, beholding as in a mirror the glory of the Lord, are being transformed into the same image from glory to glory, just as by the Spirit of the Lord." 2 Cor 3:18

"There is therefore now no condemnation to those who are in Christ Jesus, who do not walk according to the flesh, but according to the Spirit. For the law of the Spirit of life in Christ Jesus has made me free from the law of sin and death. For what the law could not do in that it was weak through the flesh, God did by sending His own Son in the likeness of sinful flesh, on account of sin: He condemned sin in the flesh, that the righteous requirement of the law might be fulfilled in us who do not walk according to the flesh but according to the Spirit. For those who live according to the flesh set their minds on the things of the flesh, but those who live according to the Spirit, the things of the Spirit. For to be carnally minded is death, but to be spiritually minded is life and peace." Romans 8:1-6

_____

_____

_____

_____

_____

_____

_____

_____

_____

_____

The Church

Pray that we would continually be transformed by the Spirit of God, becoming more like Christ in thought, word, and deed.

Pray that we would walk in step with the Spirit, living lives that are led, empowered, and directed by Him.

Pray that we would set our minds on things above— on eternal truths and heavenly priorities—rather than being distracted by the things of this world. Romans 12:2

_____

_____

_____

_____

_____

_____

_____

_____

_____

_____

_____

_____

_____

_____

_____

_____

_____

_____

The Great Commission

Pray for those who are bound by addiction which is often rooted in deep emotional pain or unresolved trauma. Many turn to substances or harmful behaviors to numb their wounds—but that is not the answer. Only Jesus can truly heal the brokenhearted and remove the pain of the past. Where there seems to be no hope, pray that they will encounter Jesus—the Life-Giver—who brings freedom, peace, and a new beginning.

Prayer for Others

If you know someone who is bound by a bad habit or addiction—whether it's substance abuse, unhealthy relationships, compulsive behaviors, or any form of bondage pray for their complete deliverance.

Pray that the power of the Holy Spirit would break every chain that holds them captive.

Declare freedom over their life, for *"He whom the Son sets free is free indeed."* John 8:36.

_____

_____

_____

_____

_____

_____

_____

_____

_____

_____

_____

_____

_____

_____

_____

_____

_____

_____

_____

"For I know the thoughts that I think toward you,' says the Lord, 'thoughts of peace and not of evil, to give you a future and a hope.'" Jeremiah 29:11 Thank God for His sovereign plan and divine direction.

Pray for faith to trust God's timing as His plans unfolds. Wait patiently!

_____

_____

_____

_____

_____

_____

_____

_____

_____

_____

_____

_____

_____

_____

_____

_____

_____

_____

_____

_____

_____

Weekly Scripture Focus

"But He was wounded for our transgressions, He was bruised for our iniquities; The chastisement for our peace was upon Him, And by His stripes we are healed." Isaiah 53:5

"Peace I leave with you; My peace I give to you; not as the world gives do I give to you. Let not your heart be troubled, neither let it be afraid." John 14:27

As your prayer begins this week, lift up praise to God for His recent provision, and repent of wrongdoing—praying on behalf of yourself, others, the Church, and your nation.

_____

_____

_____

_____

_____

_____

_____

_____

_____

_____

_____

_____

_____

_____

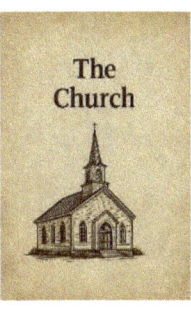

The Church

Pray that believers would fully grasp the truth that their sins have been forgiven, and they have been set free by the finished work of Christ.

Pray that they would experience the peace of God that surpasses all understanding, even in the midst of trials and difficult circumstances.

_____
_____
_____
_____
_____
_____
_____
_____
_____
_____
_____
_____
_____
_____
_____
_____
_____
_____
_____
_____
_____

The Great Commission

The Gospel has the power to change destinies. Pray that we would understand the gravity of an eternity without Christ.

Pray that we would all faithfully share the Gospel.

Pray that our testimony would be impactful and draw others to the Savior.

Ask the Holy Spirit to lead us.

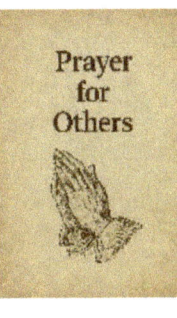

Prayer for Others

Pray for a friend and tell them you are praying for them.

Pray for their spiritual growth, blessing, and for prosperity.

Ask God to grant them the desires of their heart, if it is in line with His perfect will.

Thank Him for joy in all circumstances.

Thank God for His peace.

Thank Him for His guidance and for protection every day.

Thank Him for saving you.

_____

_____

_____

_____

_____

_____

_____

_____

_____

_____

_____

_____

_____

_____

_____

_____

_____

Weekly Scripture Focus

A Song of Ascents.

"I will lift up my eyes to the hills—from whence comes my help? My help comes from the Lord, who made heaven and earth.

He will not allow your foot to be moved; He who keeps you will not slumber. Behold, He who keeps Israel shall neither slumber nor sleep.

The Lord is your keeper; The Lord is your shade at your right hand. The sun shall not strike you by day, nor the moon by night. The Lord shall preserve you from all evil; He shall preserve your soul. The Lord shall preserve your going out and your coming in from this time forth, and even forevermore." Psalm 121:1-8

As your prayer begins this week, lift up praise to God for His recent provision, and repent of wrongdoing—praying on behalf of yourself, others, the Church, and your nation.

_____

_____

_____

_____

_____

_____

_____

_____

_____

_____

_____

_____

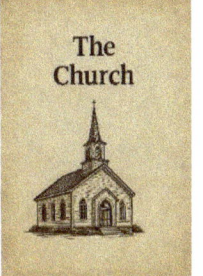

The Church

Thank the Lord:

That He is our ever-present help, our source of strength, and our refuge in every situation.

That He watches over His Church, day and night, never slumbering nor sleeping.

That He is building His Church, and the gates of Hell will not prevail against it.

His Church is triumphant.

The Great Commission

"And from the days of John the Baptist until now the kingdom of heaven suffers violence, and the violent take it by force." Matthew 11:12

In Jesus' name, push back the works of darkness.

Rebuke fear, complacency, and doubt.

Take spiritual ground through prayer, fasting, and standing on the Word of God.

Prayer for Others

Pray for single mothers who are carrying the weight of parenting alone.

Ask God to strengthen them with His peace, provision, and presence.

Pray that they will know they are not alone but deeply loved and upheld by their Heavenly Father.

Ask the Lord to surround them with a supportive community and to fill their homes with hope, wisdom, and joy as they raise their children.

_____

_____

_____

_____

_____

_____

_____

_____

_____

_____

_____

_____

_____

_____

_____

_____

_____

Keep your eyes on the Lord.

Invite Him to search your heart.

Worship Him, and thank Him for His loving kindness and love, and that His mercies are new every morning.

_____

_____

_____

_____

_____

_____

_____

_____

_____

_____

_____

_____

_____

_____

_____

_____

_____

_____

Weekly Scripture Focus

"I have set watchmen on your walls, O Jerusalem; they shall never hold their peace, day or night. You who make mention of the Lord, do not keep silent, and give Him no rest till He establishes and till He makes Jerusalem a praise in the earth."
Isaiah 62:6-7

As your prayer begins this week, lift up praise to God for His recent provision, and repent of wrongdoing—praying on behalf of yourself, others, the Church, and your nation.

_____

_____

_____

_____

_____

_____

_____

_____

_____

_____

_____

_____

_____

_____

_____

_____

_____

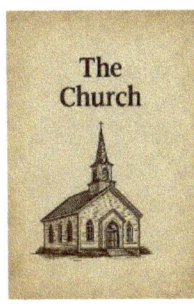

The Church

Pray that God would call His church to become "Watchmen on the Walls."

Pray that believers would be willing to embrace the cost of intercession.

Pray that we will become salt and light to those around us, carry the burdens of others, and light their way.

_____

_____

_____

_____

_____

_____

_____

_____

_____

_____

_____

_____

_____

_____

_____

_____

_____

_____

_____

The Great Commission

"But those who wait on the Lord shall renew their strength; They shall mount up with wings like eagles. They shall run and not be weary, they shall walk and not faint." Isaiah 40:31

Intercede for those who are in the Lord's field, that they do not grow weary.

Ask God to strengthen and refresh them.

_____

_____

_____

_____

_____

_____

_____

_____

_____

_____

_____

_____

_____

_____

_____

_____

_____

_____

_____

_____

_____

Prayer for Others

Pray for your family. Mention them by name.

Ask God to protect and provide for their needs.

You can be specific if you know what their needs are.

_____

_____

_____

_____

_____

_____

_____

_____

_____

_____

_____

_____

_____

_____

_____

_____

_____

_____

_____

Ask the Holy Spirit to help you persevere in prayer. To give you the kind of faith that presses through delay, silence, and opposition.

Ask the Lord to help you to not lose heart, but to always remain hopeful, believing His promises and standing firm on His Word.

Weekly Scripture Focus

"So, he answered and said to me:

"This is the word of the Lord to Zerubbabel: 'Not by might nor by power, but by My Spirit,' says the Lord of hosts. 'Who are you, O great mountain? Before Zerubbabel you shall become a plain! And he shall bring forth the capstone with shouts of Grace, grace to it.'" Zechariah 4:6-7

As your prayer begins this week, lift up praise to God for His recent provision, and repent of wrongdoing—praying on behalf of yourself, others, the Church, and your nation.

_____

_____

_____

_____

_____

_____

_____

_____

_____

_____

_____

_____

_____

_____

_____

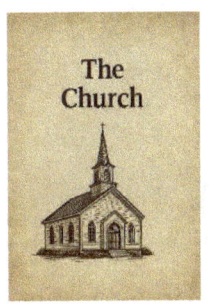

The Church

Pray that the power of the Holy Spirit would rest upon each of us in the coming year—guiding, strengthening, and equipping us to walk in God's purpose with boldness and faith.

Thank God for His abundant grace that has sustained us, and continues to keep us, His unfailing mercy that forgives us, His overflowing joy that strengthens us, His perfect peace that guards our hearts, and His steadfast love that never fails.

The Great Commission

Pray for the multitudes who stand in "The Valley of Decision," unsure of which path to take. The year is over, and time is running out.

Pray that the Gospel be proclaimed boldly, clearly, and without compromise—piercing through confusion, doubt, and spiritual darkness.

Pray that every word spoken, every action taken, and every ministry effort be led and empowered by the Spirit of the Lord, bringing conviction, transformation, and salvation, as we redeem the time. Jesus is coming soon.

_____

_____

_____

_____

_____

_____

_____

_____

_____

_____

_____

_____

_____

_____

_____

_____

Prayer for Others

Pray for single parents who are doing their best to lead, provide, and nurture their children.

Ask God to give them wisdom, strength, and grace for each day.

Pray that they will rely on the Lord as their source of guidance and encouragement.

Pray for support systems to come alongside them, and for their children to flourish under their care.

_____

_____

_____

_____

_____

_____

_____

_____

_____

_____

_____

_____

_____

_____

_____

_____

_____

Thank God for His amazing grace that reached into your darkness, lifted you out, and set your feet on the path of hope and purpose.

Praise Him for the future He has prepared for you, and for the light of His love that now guides your way.

Thank Him for bringing you through this year and the many blessings upon your life.

_____

_____

_____

_____

_____

_____

_____

_____

_____

_____

_____

_____

_____

_____

_____

_____

_____

_____

Epilogue

"Now to Him who is able to do exceedingly abundantly more than all we ask or think, according to His power that works in us, to Him be glory in the church by Christ Jesus
to all generations, forever and ever, Amen." Ephesians 3:20–21

For fifty-two weeks, you have walked through Scripture, prayer, and reflection. Each page has been a step of faith, a seed planted, and a moment recorded before the Lord. Completing this journal is not simply reaching the end of a book—it is a testimony of God's faithfulness and your perseverance.

But this is not the end of your prayer journey. These pages were meant to train your heart to walk daily with God, to intercede for others, and to live watchfully and expectantly. What you have begun here is meant to overflow into a lifelong rhythm of prayer.

The prayers you've prayed are not forgotten. They rise before God like incense (Revelation 5:8). Some have already been answered; others are still unfolding in God's perfect time. None of your words have been wasted. Heaven has recorded them, and eternity will reveal their impact.

So, as you close this journal, open another for your journey this coming year. Continue to lift your eyes to Jesus, the Author and Finisher of your faith. Keep interceding, keep seeking, keep believing, it is the breath of your walk with God.

May the Lord bless you and keep you.
May His presence go before you and His glory rest upon you.
May your prayers shape nations, change lives, and draw you ever closer to His heart.
And may the flame of intercession never grow dim within you, until that day when faith becomes sight, and prayer gives way to eternal praise.

This journal ends, but prayer continues.